SHE SPEAKS

About the Author

Yvette Cooper is the Labour MP for Normanton, Pontefract, Castleford and Knottingley. She served as a minister and then Cabinet minister in the 1997–2000 Labour Government, including as Chief Secretary to the Treasury and Secretary of State for Work and Pensions. She was the first Cabinet minister to take maternity leave and has campaigned on issues from child poverty and economic regeneration to online abuse and child refugees. Since 2016 she has been chair of the Home Affairs Select Committee. She is also a mum, a terrible but enthusiastic gardener, and enjoys overly competitive family sports.

SHE SPEAKS

WOMEN'S SPEECHES THAT CHANGED THE WORLD, FROM PANKHURST TO THUNBERG

YVETTE COOPER

Atlantic Books
London

First published in hardback in Great Britain in 2019 by Atlantic Books, an imprint of Atlantic Books Ltd.

This paperback edition published in 2020

10 9 8

A CIP catalogue record for this book is available from the British Library.

Internal illustrations © Anna Higgie
Text design by www.benstudios.co.uk

Paperback ISBN: 978 1 78649 994 3
E-book ISBN: 978 1 78649 995 0

Printed in Great Britain

Atlantic Books
An imprint of Atlantic Books Ltd
Ormond House
26–27 Boswell Street
London
WC1N 3JZ

www.atlantic-books.co.uk

CONTENTS

Preface to the Paperback Edition

Women's voices have been sidelined for too long. It's time to fight back – to promote, debate and celebrate the public words of women through the ages and across the world. That is why I put together this collection of women's speeches – to tell the stories of the incredible women behind them, to inspire readers, and to encourage more women to speak out.

In the hardback edition, published in November 2019, I argued that spoken words matter, speeches matter, that they are pathways to power. When women's voices are not heard, it undermines democracy and hurts us all. I challenged the speech anthologies, public events and conference line-ups that still carry so few women's words, and chronicled the attempts to silence women, both today and throughout history.

A few short months later, as I write these words for the paperback edition, everything has changed and nothing has changed. The world has been turned upside down by the COVID-19 global pandemic. Things once unimaginable have come to pass, with the heartbreaking loss of so many lives, with families kept apart, and with schools, workplaces and community centres closed to keep people safe. For months, the public forums for speeches have been silent. It is poignant to think of the words not spoken as weddings and wakes were put on hold; sports games, political rallies, conferences and graduation ceremonies were cancelled; and religious sermons were suspended. We have had to learn new ways to reach out and connect with each other, applauding key workers from doorsteps and balconies, speaking and meeting online. Even Parliament closed temporarily, and I could never have imagined that I would make a speech to the House of Commons whilst sitting at home in an upstairs room, staring into Zoom.

But the crisis has also shown the power of words and highlighted the importance of ensuring that diverse voices are heard. This year, speeches have held the power of life and death. Without drugs or vaccines to protect us from the spread of this deadly virus, politicians, scientists, doctors and public figures have had to use the power of persuasion to convince us to make the personal sacrifices necessary to protect each other, and to explain how much is at stake – words have saved lives.

In the midst of all this turbulence we have seen both inspiring examples of women's leadership and oratory in some parts of the world, and a troubling absence of women's voices in others. Sadly, here in the UK, in the words from the heart of government, women have been marginalized. Throughout the peak of the first wave, government ministers made daily short speeches to update and advise the public through virtual press conferences. A shocking eighty-nine out of the ninety-two ministerial speeches were made by men; only 30 per cent of the members of the key scientific advisory committee are women. The UK government has been criticized for lack of transparency and lack of empathy, both in its decision-making and its public communication – the absence of diverse views and voices has weakened the national response.

When looking for a British speech that encapsulated the crisis to add to this paperback edition, I could not find anything from our government. Instead, the most powerful unifying words, spoken when things felt darkest in early April, came from the Queen. In a very unusual televised address, the 96-year-old monarch drew upon our national history to evoke a sense of resilience and compassion, praising the 'quiet good-humoured resolve and fellow-feeling' that characterizes our communities.

At the same time, across the world, some of the women whose earlier speeches already feature in this book have been applauded again for their words and for their leadership in the face of this global emergency. New Zealand Prime Minister Jacinda Ardern and German Chancellor Angela Merkel have both been widely praised for their approach to the crisis and for the way they have communicated with their countries throughout the pandemic, building trust through empathy, honesty and clarity, and taking firm action to keep the loss of life down. The words Ardern chose when addressing the people of New Zealand differed starkly from the war-like language of 'battle' and 'invisible enemies' used ubiquitously by male leaders across the globe: 'Be kind to each other,' she said, mobilizing a sense of solidarity and responsibility among her listeners.

Several other speeches from among the thirty-five included in the first edition also feel more important than ever at this time. Words from the speech by civil rights activist and poet Audre Lourde, given in Chicago in 1977, have been emblazoned on the banners of Black Lives Matter protesters – her words, 'your silence will not protect you', are resonating with activists around the world and feel relevant and rousing for a new generation. This year, in response to the racist murder of George Floyd in the US, we have seen an important and long-overdue public acknowledgement of the responsibility we all bear to recognize and challenge racism and injustice wherever we find it, and to seek out under-represented voices, to amplify them and to learn from them. Lupita Nyong'o's speech, included in this collection, is a powerful, personal reflection on how it feels to be judged by the colour of your skin. Here in the UK, the words and actions many decades ago of trade unionist Joan O'Connell and Labour stalwart Barbara Castle, both included in this book, once again feel relevant this year as we mark the fiftieth anniversary of the implementation of the Equal Pay Act, at a time when women face new job losses, pay cuts and childcare pressures as a result of the COVID-19 crisis. Meanwhile, Diane Abbott's speech on the Windrush scandal continues to echo, as victims have not received the support and compensation they need. Back in Castleford Queens Mill in my constituency, as we have been delivering books, food parcels and activities to local residents during these difficult times, I have thought often of Alison Drake, our local champion whose speeches and campaigning first started our vital community network of volunteers at the Mill. And as we try to rebuild our economies in a better way after this crisis, we must remember Greta Thunberg's call for action on the climate emergency.

Lilit Martirosyan's words on violence against trans women aren't just about her experience in Armenia but reflect evidence from across the world of continuing violence and threats against transgender people everywhere. And while nations across the globe feel fraught and divided, Jo Cox's words still remind us that we have more in common than that which divides us.

Sadly, the experience of violence and threats, and the attempts to silence women, have continued. Angry tirades by online trolls continue without any sign of abating. Women ministers in Italy and Austria have had to seek police protection this year in the face of threats. Meghan Markle was the target of sexism and racism in the media and online before she left the UK. At the 2019 UK general election, which coincided with the first publication of this book, several women MPs stood down, saying they were no longer prepared to tolerate the vitriol and abuse. Soon afterwards a Conservative activist in my constituency was jailed for making a violent threat towards me.

The women in this book have refused to be silenced. Their determination has inspired me to find even more speeches to add to this paperback edition – and their struggles are not over. Manal al-Sharif spearheaded the movement for women's right to drive in Saudi Arabia, but she lives in exile, while other women campaigners in Saudi Arabia have been imprisoned without trial – a stark reminder that some of the battles for women's human rights have not yet been won. I listened in Parliament to Rosie Duffield's deeply moving and personal speech about domestic abuse and I know it has already given comfort and confidence to women across the country at a time when domestic abuse has been on the rise. I have also included US footballer Megan Rapinoe's uplifting team talk – a reminder to be bold, brave and, above all, kind. Words have most power when they are believed and trusted, so at a time when facts themselves feel under threat from those promoting conspiracy theories and fake news online, I was particularly keen to include Marie Colvin – the brave and remarkable war correspondent who died in pursuit of truth – and her speech from 2010 on the importance of journalists bearing witness.

In the months I spent researching this book, I came across so many brilliant speeches by formidable women and so many fascinating stories behind them that I struggled to choose only forty to include. This is not a definitive list of the all-time greatest speeches by women; rather, it is a compilation of powerful voices that have influenced and inspired me, that have helped build movements and deliver change. There are many, many more that could have been included in these pages. I urge you to seek them out, to find the ones that resonate with you and which represent you, and to share them with others. It is only by finding and amplifying the words of women that we can ensure that the power of our voices continues to reverberate through the generations.

I hope discovering and delving into these speeches will be as meaningful and inspiring for you as it has been for me.

Yvette Cooper
Castleford, July 2020

'Where the words of women are crying to be heard,
we must each of us recognize our responsibility to seek those
words out, to read them and share them'

Audre Lorde

Introduction

For centuries, brave and bold women have spoken out. They have used their voices to rally communities and crowds, to persuade, to teach and to inspire change. But too often their words have been lost or drowned out and their powerful interventions omitted from history. Too often they've had to fight to be heard while others tried to silence them.

Speeches have been part of my working life for over twenty years, but when I've searched other speeches for inspiration, in anthologies or online, I've been amazed by how women disappear. Most collections of speeches include few women. You could be forgiven for thinking that Elizabeth I was the only woman in history to make a speech – and even her words were written down later by a man. Today, although there are far more women involved in politics, public services and business, women are still less likely to speak or be heard from a public stage, less likely to speak or be heard at conferences or in meetings.

This book fights back. It's a celebration of speeches by women from across the world and across the centuries – brilliant battle cries, passionate polemics and reflective ruminations. These are speeches from warrior queens and world leaders, teenagers and pensioners, celebrity activists and local community champions. And they talk about everything from physics to prostitution, war to beauty.

For several years I have wanted to put this book together – hoping that some of the speeches that have inspired me will inspire both women and men and will also encourage more women to speak in public. After all, leadership and authority often depend on public speech – whether it be in politics or the workplace, at community events or office presentations, even weddings and funerals. So if women aren't speaking or being heard, they will often be kept out of positions of power too.

It feels even more important to promote women's speeches now. First, because we are in great need of more thoughtful, creative and passionate speeches from the widest range of people possible. Right now in our public debates, there is so much shouting, and too little speaking and listening. Politics is a maelstrom, there's a culture war online, and the pace of changes in technology, population and climate means that no one has all the answers and we need more voices to be heard. Second, because while more women are now claiming the stage and speaking publicly, many also face a dangerous backlash and are targeted with vitriol and even violence. Some of those who try to speak out are being hounded instead of heard. They face deliberate attempts to intimidate them into silence.

When women parliamentarians from over 100 countries gathered at Westminster to mark the 2018 centenary of the first UK women's votes, most of them had stories to tell of bullying, abuse and threats. Women outside politics who've led campaigns or become public figures can face organized trolling and targeted abuse designed to keep them quiet.

Most shocking of all is when the misogyny comes not just from keyboard warriors but from the most powerful man in the world.

The President of the United States encourages huge crowds to chant against women politicians: for Hillary Clinton, the cry was 'lock her up'; for Congresswoman Ilhan Omar it was 'send her back'. He has called women 'dogs', 'fat pigs' and 'slobs', and set the tone from the top for waves of threats and abuse not just targeted at female politicians but towards women more widely.

Here in the UK, women MPs routinely receive death threats or rape threats – and the abuse is much worse for black, Muslim or Jewish women. I know talented women who are giving up politics because of it. In the House of Commons Labour MPs sit beneath a coat of arms painted for our colleague Jo Cox, murdered three years ago for doing her job.

Even five years ago, I could not have imagined any of this happening. I could never have imagined losing a friend to such violence. I would never have dreamed when I first became an MP that there would be weeks when my office would have to report thirty-five different threats to the police, when some would be so serious that arrests would follow, or when fellow human beings I have never met would call for me to be beaten, shot or strung up because they didn't like something I'd said. None of this is normal. We must never treat it as so.

Hence this book. Instead of letting brilliant women be silenced, I wanted more and more people to hear their voices and their words. As I searched for different speeches, I came across wonderful, inspiring stories which show how speeches can change minds and change lives. I also uncovered tales that show the obstacles women have had to overcome. And I found shocking evidence that the backlash against women who speak out isn't new. But nor, thankfully, is the bravery of strong women who persist and overcome.

THE POWER OF SPEECH

My dad taught me how to make speeches and gave me the confidence to speak out. He was a trade unionist who spoke up for his members' rights at conferences and on shop floors, persuading crowds when to get angry and fight, or when to calm down because this was the best deal they were going to get. He told me about the speeches he made, how he wrote his arguments down in longhand, then a second time just as notes, and how he always aimed to speak from memory not from a text. I listened.

For over twenty years, public speaking has been part of my work and my life. I've made good speeches, bad speeches, funny speeches, waffly speeches and speeches that were frankly just deadly dull. Each speech can be a fresh nervous moment. Each one can be fraught. I've given speeches in the oddest of circumstances, sometimes with one of our children holding onto my skirt, running round the back of the hall or heckling. For years my husband Ed Balls and I had to make major speeches in parallel at Labour Party Conference – we would take it in turns to practise reading from an ironing board propped up as a makeshift lectern in the Conference hotel, rewriting each others' perorations or jokes. One year I decided to delete a line about clamping down on anti-social behaviour after he returned from the annual Conference football match between MPs and the media having managed to elbow a journalist in the eye.

My worst moments involved misjudging my audience. On one occasion, opening a new school extension, I rattled on for far too long about the importance of education until an impatient seven-year-old ran up and pulled open the curtain behind me. The parents applauded loudly and a wave of relief spread through the room.

I became a Labour MP in 1997 because of a speech. We were in a packed main hall in Castleford High School at the local Labour selection meeting. I was just twenty-eight years old, there were several older men on the panel, and no one – including me – expected me to be selected as the candidate. But I spoke as my dad had taught me – from the notes I'd remembered and from my heart, not from a text.

I remember starting by talking about the Castleford High School pupils who would shortly be taking their exams in that hall and who needed an MP ready to fight for their future. I talked about my grandad who had been a miner, like many of the men in the hall. And I talked about the values that led me to join the Labour Party and the better future that a Labour government could bring. Party members told me afterwards it was the speech that did it – they changed their minds, decided to support me and eight weeks later, still in a bit of a state of shock, I entered Parliament as the Pontefract and Castleford MP.

Since then, I've seen how speeches can change people's minds and people's lives. Public debate is the lifeblood of democracy – the use of words not swords to change a nation. Spoken words can heal and unite communities or whip up anger and spread poison.

Speeches hold power, but not just in politics. They mark out the milestones in our lives – the wedding tributes, the retirement drinks, the funeral orations. Even towards the end of the Last Night of the Proms, I look forward to the conductor's short speech – watching to see how the sentences dance between the music, and how they move the crowd. TED Talks have brought in new audiences as millions of people have watched online some of the most popular fifteen-minute talks on everything from body language to space travel.

And from the sports captain's team talk to the corporate manager's PowerPoint presentation, we use them to steer and guide, to mark authority and to lead.

WHERE ARE THE WOMEN?

When speeches have so much power, it really matters that women are missing. Despite all the speeches I've made over the years, and despite the growing numbers of women in leadership positions, public speaking can still feel like a man's world.

As we approach 2020, women are still less likely to hold public office, less likely to speak at private conferences, less likely to hold forth in a conference call. Even in recent anthologies or online celebrations of oratory, women are still notably absent – often accounting for just one in five or even fewer than one in ten of the chosen speeches.

For women breaking into traditionally male spheres, making speeches can be daunting. To hold an audience's attention, you have to be confident in your authority but also feel something in common with those who are listening – all things which are harder if you are talking to an all-male audience. Harriet Harman has described speaking in Parliament in the 1980s when there were hardly any women and hearing the grumbling from all sides when she dared to stand up and talk about childcare. Even by the time I was elected with more women in 1997, I would often find myself facing Conservative opposition benches entirely filled with rows of chuntering men.

I remember being asked as a junior health minister to speak at a Labour Press Conference during the 2001 General Election with the Prime Minister (Tony Blair), Chancellor (Gordon Brown) and

Health Secretary (Alan Milburn). Rightly, the party had realized that holding an all-male press conference wasn't a great look. Heavily pregnant, I dutifully travelled down from Yorkshire to attend. But when I arrived, it became clear that no one actually expected me to speak or had any announcements or points for me to make. Nor did they expect me to answer questions from any of the journalists. I had to insist on speaking, and then I had to interrupt Tony Blair in order to get in an answer – feeling hugely embarrassed about doing so, but even more embarrassed about just sitting in silence on the stage.

The *Penguin Book of Historic Speeches* published in the mid-1990s offered the following explanation for the pitifully few women's speeches it included:

> There are three reasons. One is that ... until the mid twentieth century few featured on the great stages. Another, given by some feminists, is that women have wanted no part in the macho game of domination by speech. The third is physical – women's voices are not made by nature for oratory. They are not deep enough.

But this is ludicrous. The idea that women's voices just aren't manly enough to make a speech is circular nonsense. Tell that to the women whose TED Talks have been watched and enjoyed by millions – like Chimamanda Ngozi Adichie, whose speech is included in this volume. Women make up ten out of the top twenty-five most popular TED Talks online. Their higher vocal range hasn't stopped audiences enjoying or being fascinated by their words.

Yes, it is true that until recently there have been few women prime ministers, presidents or Nobel Prize winners, but concentrating only on the great stages or offices of state means missing the powerful speeches made by women in church halls or assembly rooms or shop floors. Admittedly some of those speeches are harder to find and often weren't written down. It took me longer to find recorded speeches from some of the early women trade unionists and even more recent women community activists. But just because many of their words weren't written down it doesn't mean women weren't speaking out.

Nor does it mean those speeches were less important than the words of kings and princes. Many of the speeches I've chosen capture movements rather than moments. The speeches by the abolitionists, the suffragettes, the campaigners against extremism, or the environmentalists, have changed minds and changed lives. Unlike prime ministers and presidents on great stages, none of them on their own had the power to change the course of a country, but together they did something even harder and more important, they built movements – speech after speech, touring towns and cities, persuading strangers, spreading their words online – and the movements were more powerful than any one leader's speech alone could ever be.

There are countless stories of trailblazing women speaking up and speaking out, not on the great stages but around them and behind them. I found many of them in the course of my search and included them here, but there are millions more – by women we've heard of and women we haven't. They shouldn't be forgotten or pushed to the periphery anymore. It's time to put them centre stage.

As for the idea that it is women's fault for rejecting the chance to join the male tradition of making speeches, that is nonsense too. That Penguin anthology was written the same year that Hillary Clinton declared at the United Nations that 'women's rights are human rights', and that Benazir Bhutto spoke to the United Nations as the first woman ever elected to head an Islamic nation. Women haven't shunned public speech, but for centuries many of them have been kept out altogether.

Growing up in Britain in the seventies, most of the early speeches I heard were given by men; headteachers in school assemblies, politicians on TV, vicars at church and local mayors at summer fetes. For centuries, the main oratorical traditions – for political and civic leaders to their constituencies, military leaders to their troops and religious leaders to their congregations – were mostly closed to women. From the time of the Ancient Greeks, women were excluded from public life and positions of power, the platforms on which speeches would typically be made. As Mary Beard, the authoritative classicist, wrote in her book *Women & Power*:

> Public speaking and oratory were not merely things that ancient women *didn't do*: they were exclusive practices and skills that defined masculinity as a gender.

Women's oral traditions, teaching and passing on stories through the generations, haven't been considered or counted as speeches in the same way. We don't value those public speaking traditions enough. My mum was a maths teacher. Every day she had to stand up in front of an audience of teenagers, hold their attention, keep her authority, plant ideas and persuade them daily to open their minds. Effectively she was making speeches every day – and far more frequently than my dad or I ever did in our jobs – yet no one thinks about teaching like that.

Women have also always faced the added pressure of being judged on their appearance – their clothes and hair, as well as the sound of their voices. Even the Roman historians who recorded Boudica's rousing battle cries also commented on her physical appearance and attire. I know how many times I've spent too long worrying about which jacket to wear for a speech, knowing I'll be judged on my image, as well as my words.

Fear of judgement, be it on your appearance, your voice or your words, can become paralysing. The truth is, whatever the forum, however big or small the stage, public speaking is exposure and that can always feel risky and hard. In one of my favourite speeches in this book, the poet and civil rights activist Audre Lorde argues that speaking out 'is never without fear – of visibility, of the harsh light of scrutiny and perhaps of judgement …'. But she also argues that visibility makes us stronger, that our silences will not protect us.

Even after years of making speeches, I still find them stressful and still sometimes want to run away and hide instead. If you throw your words out into the world, someone will disagree, someone will knock them down. But those words will also lift others up. Our words help us build precious personal relationships and create powerful public ones. It's how we build our communities, our cities, how we teach our children, how we instil hope and create a vision for the future.

If you believe that your words need to be said, then you can't stand back and hope someone else will say them. Whoever you are, whatever you're wearing, your voice is important.

SHE SPEAKS

I've chosen speeches for this book that move me, in the hope that they will inspire others too. They come from across the world and across the generations – from Boudica to Greta Thunberg – two thousand years apart. The book includes stories and experiences that women have widely shared, but I hope it also reflects the diversity of women's experiences rooted in class, race, sexuality or disability and the different countries, cultures and centuries in which they have lived.

They aren't all speeches that changed the world – though some did and will continue to do so – but they are speeches that inspire, encourage and intrigue. Some are beautiful, poetic and rhetorical. Others are simple. Some, like Julia Gillard's, I strongly agree with. Others, like Margaret Thatcher's, I really don't. But each speech has strength and purpose. And there were many, many more I could have chosen – limiting the selection for this book was a hard task.

Half the speeches are from Britain, the others are from across the world. Some are by national leaders like Angela Merkel and Benazir Bhutto. Some are by celebrities like Lupita Nyong'o, Emma Watson or Ellen DeGeneres. Others are by grassroots activists you have probably never heard of, like trade unionist Joan O'Connell, whose words were echoed in one of the scenes in the film *Made in Dagenham*, or my Castleford friend Alison Drake, who led a remarkable community regeneration in our coalfield town. I've included a speech from Malala when she was just sixteen years old, and a speech from Barbara Castle just before she turned ninety.

Some are difficult to read. I have included my friend Jo Cox's maiden speech, made just a year before she was killed. And perhaps the most important speech of all is the testimony from the Holocaust survivor Eva Kor about her terrible experience at Auschwitz. Kor died aged nearly ninety while I was putting this book together.

Each of these women spoke with purpose and determination. Each showed leadership and strength in the face of obstacles. And they have shown that powerful and persuasive oratory can certainly be female.

SHE WON'T BE SILENCED

There is a darker side to all these stories. As I gathered these speeches together, I was struck, and actually horrified, by the number of these brave women who have had to face serious threats, abuse or violence from those who wanted them to stay quiet. Through the centuries, those who fear women's voices have too often turned to violence or bullying to get their way. And out of the forty women in this book, most of them have faced serious threats, abuse or violence for speaking out.

Boudica was attacked and her daughters raped because she dared to speak up against Roman authority. Josephine Butler, the Victorian campaigner for women's rights, had to escape from a window when the barn she was speaking in was set on fire by her opponents. Sojourner Truth, the abolitionist, faced mobs outside the churches where she spoke. The Suffragettes were tortured and force-fed. Benazir Bhutto, Pakistan's first woman prime minister, was assassinated by the Taliban. Decades later they also shot Malala Yousafzai in the head when she spoke up for girls' education.

Wangari Maathai, the Kenyan environmentalist, was brutally beaten by the police for her peaceful activism. Julia Gillard, the former Australian prime minister, was bombarded with misogynistic abuse and violent threats. Ellen DeGeneres had death threats, bomb threats and her TV show cancelled after she came out. Diane Abbott, Britain's first black MP, personally received more than half the vitriolic abuse aimed at British MPs during the last general election. And we lost my fellow Labour MP, Jo Cox, when she was killed by a far-right extremist in 2016.

In 2019, Lilit Martirosyan had to go into hiding after death threats for being the first transgender activist to speak in the Armenian Parliament. Democrat rising star Alexandria Ocasio-Cortez was among four American congresswomen of colour told by the President of the United States to go back to where they came from, and Greta Thunberg, the sixteen-year-old climate activist, faced awful abusive online trolling for daring to speak out.

But this book is proof that women will not be silenced. The suffragettes weren't silenced. Nor were the abolitionists. Nor are today's campaigners deterred. These women's stories should be the inspiration to us to challenge the rising tide of hatred and misogyny fuelled by a minority online and offline. Because now there are more of us who are willing to speak out. And there will be more still; women who speak out, and men who support us when we do.

The women in this book wouldn't stay quiet. Their words live on after their speeches and will live on after they have gone. Because, as Jo Cox said, 'we have far more in common than that which divides us'. Because, as Michelle Obama said, 'when they go low, we go high'. And because, as Audre Lorde said, 'there are so many silences to be broken'.

Perhaps, though, the most inspiring message in all of these speeches is not about the darkness these orators have had to overcome, but about the light ahead and their optimism for a better future. From Angela Merkel's faith that we will find a door in the darkest of walls, to Maya Angelou's hopeful poem about the pulse of a new day, these are women who believe in using words to build a better world, and persuading others to join them as they do. These are women who do wonderful things. Women who do normal things. Women like all of us.

They are all women of whom I have thought – she speaks, I must listen.

BOUDICA

'A Woman's Resolve'

BATTLE OF WATLING STREET
Account by Tacitus, AD 60

Two thousand years ago, a British warrior queen made this incredible speech.

It is one of the earliest accounts we have of public oratory by any woman and it is a furious roar against violation.

Reading it, I find it astonishing that this speech was given so long ago, as many of the images and ideas attributed to Boudica have continued to echo through the centuries since, including in the speeches of other women found in this book.

After her husband died in AD 60, the Romans refused to accept Boudica or her daughters as the heirs to the lands and the regency of the Iceni tribe. She was flogged, her daughters raped, and other tribe elders were killed. The cruelty of the Romans provoked uprising among several of the Celtic tribes, and with Boudica leading them the united tribes took Colchester and London, burning buildings and killing thousands before finally being defeated somewhere in the Midlands at the battle of Watling Street.

According to Roman historian Tacitus, this is the speech Boudica gave to the gathered tribes before leading them into their final battle.

All we really know of Boudica are the stories told about her by men some years later. Cassius Dio describes her as 'very tall, in appearance most terrifying, in the glance of her eye most fierce and her voice was harsh'. Tacitus describes her riding her chariot among the united tribes, her speech a rousing battle cry.

Her words are stirring. Her fierce call for 'a righteous vengeance' against the violation of women and country would be echoed 1,500 years later by Elizabeth I in a speech to her troops at Tilbury. And her invocation of 'a woman's resolve', ready to win or die, would be seized on by the suffragettes, who used her image on their banners.

The rhetoric may owe much to Tacitus, but the legend of a female warrior leader inspiring her people, defending her daughters and her land, has become an important part of British folk history. Be she bellicose warmonger or fearless mother and queen, her story and image have been appropriated through the centuries as the Elizabethans and Victorians erected monuments to her.

By Westminster Bridge in London stands one of those monuments; a huge bronze statue of Boudica and her daughters. Arms raised to the heavens, horses tearing, hair streaming, three women charge their bronze chariot towards Big Ben – a reminder to today's campaigners and activists as they gather around Parliament of the long tradition of women roaring against injustice and turning personal pain and humiliation into a rallying cry for action.

But now,

it is not as a woman descended from noble ancestry,

but as one of the people that I am avenging lost freedom,

my scourged body,

the outraged chastity of my daughters.

Roman lust has gone so far that not our very person, nor even age or
    virginity, are left unpolluted.

But heaven is on the side of a righteous vengeance;

a legion which dared to fight has perished;

the rest are hiding themselves in their camp, or are thinking anxiously
    of flight.

They will not sustain even the din and the shout of so many
    thousands, much less our charge and our blows.

If you weigh well the strength of the armies, and the causes of the
    war, you will see that in this battle you must conquer or die.

This is a woman's resolve; as for men, they may live and be slaves.

QUEEN ELIZABETH I

'The Heart and Stomach of a King'

SPEECH TO THE TROOPS AT TILBURY

1588

Elizabeth I's speech to the troops at Tilbury was the first speech I ever read. It was the Silver Jubilee year for Queen Elizabeth II, and our small-town primary school was celebrating all things Elizabethan from the sixteenth century to the twentieth. In an old Ladybird book on Queen Elizabeth I from the school library, I found this speech. I loved it – as much for the rhythms and poetry as for the sentiment and story – and I learned it by heart.

When Elizabeth I gave this speech in 1588, she had already been queen for thirty years, but England remained divided, troubled and in fear of invasion by the mighty Spanish Armada. By the time she travelled to Tilbury, the Armada had already been driven off course after struggling against the English fleet, and the threat of invasion was starting to recede. But Elizabeth's decision to appear on horseback and address the thousands of gathering troops was clever and important.

The defeat of the Armada became a turning point for the nation's self-confidence and self-image as an emerging military power. The power of the speech – its timing, its pageantry, its words – is that it bound together Elizabeth and England's victory for ever after, entwining Elizabeth and England's strength.

There are strong echoes of Boudica's speech 1,500 years earlier: a queen seeking to inspire her troops to save her land and her people from invaders; a woman needing to establish her authority over an army of men; a speech, a spirit and an iconic image that has endured through the centuries, but with words that rely on male accounts written many years later.

Like Boudica, Elizabeth seeks first to persuade that she speaks for and with her troops – Boudica says she is 'one of the people', Elizabeth pledges 'to live and die amongst you all'. Like Boudica she invokes the images of violation and dishonour – Boudica calls for vengeance for her 'scourged body, the outraged chastity of my daughters', Elizabeth for scorn against 'dishonour' and any prince who 'dare to invade the borders of my realm'.

For Boudica the violation of the Queen is the violation of the Iceni tribe, for Elizabeth the violation of the country is the violation of the Virgin Queen. But while Boudica uses her womanhood as strength, 'this is a woman's resolve', Elizabeth turns it into strength only by showing her ability to disavow it, in her most famous line: 'I have the body but of a weak and feeble woman; but I have the heart and stomach of a king.'

This account of her speech comes from a letter from Leonel Sharp to the Duke of Buckingham over sixty-five years later. Sharp claims that these are her words, which he was instructed to repeat to the troops at the time. But even if the words themselves are not reliable, the theatre of the speech and the myths woven around it show the remarkable leader that Elizabeth I was.

My loving people,

we have been persuaded by some that are careful of our safety, to take heed how we commit our selves to armed multitudes, for fear of treachery;

but I assure you I do not desire to live to distrust my faithful and loving people.

Let tyrants fear, I have always so behaved myself that, under God, I have placed my chiefest strength and safeguard in the loyal hearts and good-will of my subjects;

and therefore I am come amongst you, as you see, at this time, not for my recreation and disport, but being resolved, in the midst and heat of the battle, to live and die amongst you all;

to lay down for my God, and for my kingdom, and my people, my honour and my blood, even in the dust.

I know I have the body but of a weak and feeble woman;

but I have the heart and stomach of a king, and of a king of England too,

and think foul scorn that Parma or Spain, or any prince of Europe, should dare to invade the borders of my realm;

to which rather than any dishonour shall grow by me, I myself will take up arms,

I myself will be your general, judge, and rewarder of every one of your virtues in the field.

I know already, for your forwardness you have deserved rewards and crowns; and We do assure you in the word of a prince, they shall be duly paid you.

In the meantime, my lieutenant general shall be in my stead, than whom never prince commanded a more noble or worthy subject;

not doubting but by your obedience to my general,

by your concord in the camp,

and your valour in the field,

we shall shortly have a famous victory over those enemies of my God, of my kingdom, and of my people.

99

SOJOURNER TRUTH

'I Am a Woman's Rights'

AKRON, OHIO

May 1851

Sojourner Truth could not read or write. But my, could she speak.

Born into slavery in New York State as Isabella Baumfree, she was sold at auction aged just nine years old. Over the first thirty years of her life, she was beaten, bought and sold many times, before she walked to freedom with her youngest daughter, but was forced to leave her other children behind.

Sojourner Truth was her chosen name. She became a passionate Christian and joined abolitionists touring the country campaigning against slavery, becoming one of their bravest and most powerful speakers – and she argued for women's rights alongside abolition. Fighting for political change at that time often meant travelling from town to town, speaking from public platforms and finding the passionate words to persuade strangers to join your cause.

It can't have been easy. Truth had already endured torture, violence, exploitation and servitude. And when she then spoke out to help others, she faced threats of violence, anger and intimidation as well as racism and discrimination. But she persisted. There are stories of angry mobs gathering at churches and halls to try to silence her – on one occasion she sang to calm them down.

This speech to the Ohio Convention in 1851 is her most famous. But this isn't the most famous version of it. This version was published a month later by her friend, the journalist Marius Robinson, in the *Anti-Slavery Bugle*,[1] with the comments, 'those can only appreciate it who saw her powerful form, her whole souled earnest gesture, and listened to her strong and truthful tones'. Given without notes, the speech is rich in the rhythms of the preacher and of the Bible that others read to her.

The more famous version, however, taught in schools and included in anthologies over many decades, was written down thirteen years later by Truth's fellow abolitionist Frances Gage. Gage's version added a southern drawl, even though Truth grew up in New York speaking Dutch; it gives Truth eight more children than she was believed to have had; it adds new rhetoric. Perhaps the southern dialect was more in keeping with people's assumptions about slavery in the south. Or perhaps it was Gage's striking rhetoric – she herself was a speaker and campaigner and her version of the speech includes the famous lines:

And ain't I a woman?

I have ploughed and planted and gathered into barns and no man could head me!

And ain't I a woman?

But powerful as Gage's language was, I've chosen Robinson's earlier, simpler version of the speech. Sojourner Truth was an extraordinary woman – her words don't need to be adorned.

I want to say a few words about this matter.

I am a woman's rights.

I have as much muscle as any man, and can do as much work as any man.

I have plowed and reaped and husked and chopped and mowed, and can any man do more than that?

I have heard much about the sexes being equal.

I can carry as much as any man, and can eat as much too, if I can get it.

I am as strong as any man that is now.

As for intellect, all I can say is, if a woman have a pint, and a man a quart – why can't she have her little pint full?

You need not be afraid to give us our rights for fear we will take too much, for we can't take more than our pint'll hold. The poor men seem to be all in confusion, and don't know what to do.

Why children, if you have woman's rights, give it to her and you will feel better. You will have your own rights, and they won't be so much trouble.

I can't read, but I can hear. I have heard the Bible and have learned that Eve caused man to sin.

Well, if woman upset the world, do give her a chance to set it right side up again.

The Lady has spoken about Jesus, how he never spurned woman from him, and she was right. When Lazarus died, Mary and Martha came to him with faith and love and besought him to raise their brother.

And Jesus wept - and Lazarus came forth. And how came Jesus into the world?

Through God who created him and the woman who bore him. Man, where is your part?

But the women are coming up blessed be God and a few of the men are coming up with them. But man is in a tight place, the poor slave is on him, woman is coming on him, he is surely between a hawk and a buzzard.

JOSEPHINE BUTLER

'A Voice in the Wilderness'

1874

To my shame, I had never heard of Josephine Butler before a chance conversation in Pontefract Museum a few years ago. There, I heard the story of her campaign during the 1871 Pontefract by-election in the first ever parliamentary election to be held by secret ballot – nearly fifty years before any women got the vote and well over a century before I was elected as Pontefract's first woman MP in 1997.

The Liberal candidate in the 1871 by-election was Hugh Childers – an incumbent seeking re-election and a supporter of the Contagious Diseases Act that Josephine Butler was determined to overturn. This law allowed women to be medically examined by force just for being accused of prostitution, and then imprisoned if they were found to be suffering from sexually transmitted infections.

Butler described it as 'steel rape' and she was appalled by the way the law was being used to control women and persecute prostitutes, while the men who were buying sex, exploiting women and spreading disease were simply ignored. She set up the Ladies National Association against the Act, helped gather thousands of signatures on petitions and toured the country, speaking at ninety-nine public meetings and rallies.

Like Sojourner Truth and the abolitionists across the water, and like the suffragettes who came after her, Butler was fighting for a voice while still being denied a vote. To build a movement she had to travel and speak before strangers, bravely seeking new audiences wherever she could find them. Her opponents used violence, threats and abuse to try to stop her. On one occasion the windows of her hotel room were smashed in. On another she was pelted with cow dung during a rally. When the by-election was called, Butler saw it as an opportunity to apply further public pressure on Parliament, rallying the women of Pontefract and challenging Childers to public debates. But her life was threatened for doing so. At a public meeting in nearby Knottingley, Childers' supporters were so determined to silence her that they started a fire in the building. Butler had to escape out of a window.

She didn't give in. She had started political campaigning after the tragic sudden death of her six-year-old daughter, driven, she said, by the 'urge to go forth and find some pain keener than my own'.[2]

Reading them now, the power of her speeches is in her ability to connect something very immediate and practical with evangelical rhetoric and passion. Like Sojourner Truth, she drew on religion and the oratory of the preacher to persuade her audience. After a testimony before the Royal Commission of 1871, a member of the committee was moved to remark: 'I am not accustomed to religious phraseology, but I cannot give you an idea of the effect produced except by saying that the spirit of God was there.'

This speech from 1874 is one of the many she gave on prostitution. Butler's long campaigns improved the lives of vulnerable women and paved the way for the suffrage movement that followed.

In 1885 her campaign against child abuse and the trafficking of young English girls led to the raising of the age of consent to sixteen. And then finally in 1886, fifteen years after the Pontefract by-election, the Contagious Diseases Act was finally repealed – with the support and the vote of Pontefract MP Hugh Childers.

The voice of one crying in the wilderness! A woman's voice and she cries among the multitude in 'this vast wilderness of men'.

Many have stopped for a moment to listen, and have then gone on their way. Women, they have said, should hold themselves aloof from questions of public morality; they should leave such things to the doctors and physiologists.

And others have listened, and have given heed. But when they have returned to their own business they have said, 'Yes, but we must beware of being too much influenced by words which are addressed to the heart only; it is so easy for a woman to carry away her audience by an appeal to sentiment. The subject which she is rash enough to discuss must be examined from every side.'

Be assured that this shall be done. But, after all, sentiment is a real power when it is enlisted in the service of truth. And therefore I would say to you, my opponents, who stand for the rights of cool reason, pay regard none the less to the stirring of your souls, and yield to the voice of conscience.

For a long time prostitution has been considered a simple material fact, which has indeed entailed serious hygienic consequences, but which could be dealt with calmly and sanely only by men who have special knowledge of the question.

Well, these experts have produced many medical dissertations, files upon files of papers of statistics, a vast literature in fact on the science and administration of prostitution, which is still far from exhausting the subject. But the public makes no inquiry as to the conclusions to which all this labour tends; it is contented to accept what it is told, and to stand by, uninterested and unconcerned, while fresh conditions and regulations are framed. Surely then it were well – since the materialistic treatment has produced this general indifference – to lead people to consider prostitution from another point of view.

The men of this generation seem to forget that this is not the first time that our century has brought to trial the evils which scourge society, and has given its verdict. It is irrelevant to remind them of the abolition of negro slavery, now, when we bring before them a new cause, a cause which affords only too close an analogy with the former one, since prostitution, no less than negro slavery, has its trade and its victims?

We are dealing in very truth with a great issue affecting all mankind, which concerns one sex as much as the other, and which must therefore appeal to that sentiment which you despise, to the soul, to moral affections, to the will. How can it be otherwise?

And now, when we put the question of prostitution from this new standpoint, two words will give the answer, two words from the mouth of a woman, speaking in the name of all women.

And these two words are – we rebel!

I grant that this is not the language of science; it is not the formula of statistics or of hygienic deduction; no – it is simply the outburst of that condemnation which has been kept voiceless through centuries under the yoke of legalized vice; it is the protest of all womanhood, a cry of horror, an appeal to justice, an appeal for a return to the laws of God, an appeal against the impure and brutal edicts of men.

Much may no doubt be said against the form of this declaration. It is not perfect, but it will serve. The sound of the trumpet which calls to battle is not perfect; all that is wanted is that its summons shall be sufficiently piercing to hasten the fighters into the field. So soon as they are there, the struggle will begin along the whole line.

Then will be the moment to bring up the heavy artillery and the great battalions, to destroy the enemy's works, to push him to his last entrenchment, to leave him no single road of escape.

Immense as is the task before us, nothing shall ever shatter our faith. The justice of our cause is our surety of success. At the very outset of our enterprise we hail the certain end, certain perhaps at no distant date, certain at least in that future of which we dream for our children.

And so these few words are only an appeal. But so soon as the slave grows restless and seeks to break his chains, the hour of freedom is near. All that has been wanted until now has been a voice to give the signal. Oppressed women have needed to find this voice in one of their own sex.

She is here, and she comes to proclaim uprising and deliverance. She accepts her heavy mission; she knows its burden by the numberless sufferings which she has witnessed; by the pangs – the inexpressible pangs – through which she has passed during her long years of preparation. And now the moment has come for action.

EMMELINE PANKHURST

'Freedom or Death'

HARTFORT, CONNECTICUT

November 1913

The committee rooms and corridors of the British Parliament have many great and grand portraits of men. But few of women, and barely any of the suffragettes who fought so hard for women's voices to be heard in Parliament.

So in 2013 I hung a huge framed portrait of suffragette leader Emmeline Pankhurst over the old fireplace in my parliamentary office. It's a copy of an extraordinary photo-mosaic portrait by the artist Charlotte Newson, made up of 10,000 tiny individual images of inspiring 'Women Like You' sent in by people from around the world.[3]

And it's a great tribute both to Pankhurst, and to the many mothers, daughters, sisters, neighbours, friends and heroes that

Newson incorporates into the picture – the women whose civil rights Pankhurst fought for over a century ago.

Born in Moss Side in Manchester in 1858, Pankhurst became a leading suffrage campaigner and founded the Women's Social and Political Union to campaign for the right to vote. But faced with immense resistance in Parliament and with progress slow, their tactics became more impatient and more militant. Suffragettes would smash windows and destroy property, and when imprisoned would hunger strike. Many, like Pankhurst, were arrested on multiple occasions.[4]

Pankhurst was a brilliant orator who spoke passionately and usually without notes – but it is hard to imagine this speech can have been unscripted, it is so effectively and tightly argued. It was given on a tour of America to raise money and support, between periods of imprisonment. And as well as being a great speech, it is fascinating for the insight it gives into the suffragettes' strategy and experience.

Unlike Sojourner Truth's speech, Pankhurst's is not aimed at persuading her audience to support the principle of equal suffrage. Instead it focuses on why the suffragettes have 'adopted revolutionary methods' – using different images and stories to connect with her audience, from US political history to crying babies:

> That is the whole history of politics. You have to make more noise than anybody else.

Then, in place of a moral argument in favour of women's votes, Pankhurst makes a political one – that this is a civil war, waged by women who cannot in the end be beaten because we are everywhere, and because government depends on consent.

Pankhurst vividly describes the appalling torture and force-feeding inflicted by the British state on suffragettes to try to break them, but also the remarkable strength and determination of women who lost their liberty and their health but refused to give in.

Five years after Pankhurst made this speech, the Representation of the People Act finally gave some women the right to vote in 1918, and full suffrage followed in 1928.[5] The British Parliament today is still male dominated, but nearly a third of MPs are women, and the progress we've made is only because of the bravery and battles won by women over a century ago.

I am here as a soldier who has temporarily left the field of battle in order to explain – it seems strange it should have to be explained – what civil war is like when civil war is waged by women. I am not only here as a soldier temporarily absent from the field at battle; I am here – and that, I think, is the strangest part of my coming – I am here as a person who, according to the law courts of my country, it has been decided, is of no value to the community at all; and I am adjudged because of my life to be a dangerous person, under sentence of penal servitude in a convict prison. […]

Suppose the men of Hartford had a grievance, and they laid that grievance before their legislature, and the legislature obstinately refused to listen to them, or to remove their grievance, what would be the proper and the constitutional and the practical way of getting their grievance removed? Well, it is perfectly obvious at the next general election the men of Hartford would turn out that legislature and elect a new one.

But let the men of Hartford imagine that they were not in the position of being voters at all, that they were governed without their consent being obtained, that the legislature turned an absolutely deaf ear to their demands, what would the men of Hartford do then? They couldn't vote the legislature out. They would have to choose; they would have to make a choice of two evils: they would either have to submit indefinitely to an unjust state of affairs, or they would have to rise up and adopt some of the antiquated means by which men in the past got their grievances remedied. [...]

It is about eight years since the word militant was first used to describe what we were doing. It was not militant at all, except that it provoked militancy on the part of those who were opposed to it. ... We were determined to press this question of the enfranchisement of women to the point where we were no longer to be ignored by the politicians.

You have two babies very hungry and wanting to be fed. One baby is a patient baby, and waits indefinitely until its mother is ready to feed it. The other baby is an impatient baby and cries lustily, screams and kicks and makes everybody unpleasant until it is fed. Well, we know perfectly well which baby is attended to first. That is the whole history of politics. You have to make more noise than anybody else, you have to make yourself more obtrusive than anybody else, you have to fill all the papers more than anybody else, in fact you have to be there all the time and see that they do not snow you under. [...]

If you are dealing with an industrial revolution, if you get the men and women of one class rising up against the men and women of another class, you can locate the difficulty; if there is a great industrial strike, you know exactly where the violence is and how the warfare is going to be waged; but in our war against the government you can't locate it. We wear no mark; we belong to every class; we permeate every class of the community from the highest to the lowest; and so you see in the woman's civil war the dear men of my country are discovering it is absolutely impossible to deal with it: you cannot locate it, and you cannot stop it.

'Put them in prison,' they said, 'that will stop it.' But it didn't stop it at all: instead of the women giving it up, more women did it, and more and more and more women did it until there were 300 women at a time, who had not broken a single law, only 'made a nuisance of themselves' as the politicians say.

Then they began to legislate. The British government has passed more stringent laws to deal with this agitation than it ever found necessary during all the history of political agitation in my country. They were able to deal with the revolutionaries of the Chartists' time; they were able to deal with the trades union agitation; they were able to deal with the revolutionaries later on when the Reform Acts were passed: but the ordinary law has not sufficed to curb insurgent women. They had to dip back into the Middle Ages to find a means of repressing the women in revolt.

They have said to us, government rests upon force, the women haven't force, so they must submit. Well, we are showing them that government does not rest upon force at all: it rests upon consent. As long as women consent to be unjustly governed, they can be, but directly women say: 'We withhold our consent, we will not be governed any longer so long as that government is unjust.' Not by the forces of civil war can you govern the very weakest woman. You can kill that woman, but she escapes you then; you cannot govern her. No power on earth can govern a human being, however feeble, who withholds his or her consent.

When they put us in prison at first, simply for taking petitions, we submitted; we allowed them to dress us in prison clothes; we allowed them to put us in solitary confinement; we allowed them to put us amongst the most degraded of criminals; we learned of some of the appalling evils of our so-called civilization that we could not have learned in any other way. It was valuable experience, and we were glad to get it.

I have seen men smile when they heard the words 'hunger strike', and yet I think there are very few men today who would be prepared to adopt a 'hunger strike' for any cause. It is only people who feel an intolerable sense of oppression who would adopt a means of that kind. It means you refuse food until you are at death's door, and then the authorities have to choose between letting you die and letting you go; and then they let the women go.

Now, that went on so long that the government felt that they were unable to cope. It was [then] that, to the shame of the British government, they set the example to authorities all over the world of feeding sane, resisting human beings by force. There may be doctors in this meeting: if so, they know it is one thing to feed by force an insane person; but it is quite another thing to feed a sane, resisting human being who resists with every nerve and with every fibre of her body the indignity and the outrage of forcible feeding. Now, that was done in England, and the government thought they had crushed us. But they found that it did not quell the agitation, that more and more women came in and even passed that terrible ordeal, and they were obliged to let them go. [...]

Well, they little know what women are. Women are very slow to rouse, but once they are aroused, once they are determined, nothing on earth and nothing in heaven will make women give way; it is impossible. … There are women lying at death's door, recovering enough strength to undergo operations, who have not given in and won't give in, and who will be prepared, as soon as they get up from their sick beds, to go on as before. There are women who are being carried from their sick beds on stretchers into meetings. They are too weak to speak, but they go amongst their fellow workers just to show that their spirits are unquenched, and that their spirit is alive, and they mean to go on as long as life lasts.

Now, I want to say to you who think women cannot succeed, we have brought the government of England to this position, that it has to face this alternative: either women are to be killed or women are to have the vote. I ask American men in this meeting, what would you say if in your state you were faced with that alternative, that you must either kill them or give them their citizenship? Well, there is only one answer to that alternative, there is only one way out – you must give those women the vote. […]

You have left it to women in your land, the men of all civilized countries have left it to women to work out their own salvation. That is the way in which we women of England are doing. Human life for us is sacred, but we say if any life is to be sacrificed it shall be ours; we won't do it ourselves, but we will put the enemy in the position where they will have to choose between giving us freedom or giving us death.

So here am I. I come in the intervals of prison appearance. … Probably going back to be re-arrested as soon as I set my foot on British soil. I come to ask you to help to win this fight. If we win it, this hardest of all fights, then, to be sure, in the future it is going to be made easier for women all over the world to win their fight when their time comes.

"

ELEANOR RATHBONE

'An Insult to Mothers'

HOUSE OF COMMONS

March 1945

When Eleanor Rathbone rose to speak in the British House of Commons welfare debate in March 1945, she was on the brink of a hard-won victory in the long campaign for women's financial independence and the fight against child poverty. The arguments she made were successful that day – and they also paved the way for similar fights that women MPs, including myself, have held with different governments ever since.

Rathbone and other women MPs had been arguing since the end of the First World War that the value of women's work and caring in the home should be recognized by the state, that the distribution of economic power within the family mattered and that the traditional view of the man as the head of the household should be challenged and not reinforced. So when the government brought forward plans to pay the new family allowance to the father instead of the mother, Rathbone launched a furious campaign to get this changed.

One of only fourteen women MPs in Parliament at the time, Rathbone, who was an independent MP, joined forces with Labour's Edith Summerskill and the Tories' Nancy Astor in a cross-party rebellion. They made passionate speeches at public meetings, rallies and in Parliament, maintaining the pressure until the government agreed to a free vote in March 1945.

Eleanor Rathbone's speech that day was a classic of her style – witty and powerfully argued, skilfully debunking her opponent's arguments one by one. She lists each of the government's claims in turn – that the man is 'normally the head of the household', that the law holds him responsible for the children's maintenance, that it's the normal way of things – and destroys them with wit, humour, controlled fury and forensic evidence.

But for me, the importance of her speech lies not in her power of persuasion or rhetorical devices but in the fact that her words and her campaigns have been echoed so many times since. More than half a century later, I and other women MPs have had similar arguments with successive governments, raising the same wallet and purse issues, in the same campaign for women's economic independence and against child poverty.

In 1998, when the Labour government introduced child tax credits, the Treasury proposed paying the money to the main earner instead of the main carer, and I was one of a group of newly elected Labour women backbench MPs who intervened to get it changed.

In 2010, when the Coalition government introduced Universal

Credit, they insisted on a single household payment – again, potentially undermining women's financial independence and security, especially in cases of domestic violence or coercive control. It has taken us nine years of campaigning to force the government to accept that payments should normally be made to the main carer instead.

Rathbone won the vote on family allowance that day in the House of Commons – giving many mothers some basic independent income for the first time, with a huge impact on women's independence and on reducing child poverty. It is frustrating that we still have to keep making Eleanor Rathbone's arguments, but testimony to her that she had such an impact and has shaped the debate for generations since.

The proposal, in the way it is stated in the Bill, will not raise the status of motherhood but will actually lower it.

It does so, whatever people may say, because it treats the wife as a mere appendage, which means literally a hanger on, of her husband, and gives her a very strong motive for going out to work, however much the children under her care require her presence, because then her wages will be legally her own, rather than continuing at home to bear more children.

In the words of the Bill, where the man and wife are living together the allowance will belong to the man, and that will be so even if the wife earns every penny of the income.

If the man is a rotter or a total invalid and the wife is the sole wage-earner, the allowance belongs to the man. It belongs to him if the children are hers by a first marriage. It belongs to him if they are illegitimate children.

I think I am right in saying that even if the children live with some other relative, if one or the other parent contributes to their support, he will be able to count the children as his and claim the allowance, though he may not have seen them, or even not know their Christian names.

Further, this extraordinary arrangement can only be changed by appeal to the court. But how many women will dare to appeal to the court? The worse the husband is the less will the wife dare to do so. [...]

The wife is allowed, under the Bill, to draw it, but obviously only if the man consents, because the order comes to him, and it belongs to him, so that he will hold on to it if he wants to do so.

Is that not a really amazing proposal, and what is the excuse for it? What is the reason?

The explanation given in the White Paper is that the man is normally the head of the household. Yes, normally, but the Bill gives him the money even if the wife is the sole provider.

Even otherwise, where the husband does provide the housekeeping money, what does the wife do? She merely risks her life to bring the children into the world, often with agonizing pain, and in the vast majority of working-class homes, she spends her days and hours, as they say in my part of the world, 'All the hours God makes', in washing and cleaning for the children, clothing them and feeding them – all the hours of the day and night.

School holidays and the weekends bring her no remission, no time off; they actually increase the burden on the working-class mother. All that is to go for nothing, because the law holds that the man is normally the wage earner. […]

The last defence is that it will not make any real difference; that if the man is greedy or selfish he will appropriate the money anyhow, and that if it does not come to him he will merely deduct that amount from what he allows his wife.

That shows very little knowledge of human nature. For one man who is really greedy and unscrupulous there are half a dozen who are merely weak, and creatures of habit, who hold on to what is given to them. If the money is given to the mother, and if they know that the law regards it as the child's property, or the mother's property to be spent for the child, that will help them to realize that the State recognizes the status of motherhood. […]

It is not as though there were no precedents. A woman draws maternity benefit, even if the man has been the contributor. Under the Old Age Pensions Act, old age pension is paid to the wife if she requests it. Then the allowance for evacuated children is always paid to the mother, not to the male head of the household.

In New South Wales an Act has been in operation for over twenty years, New Zealand has had one for about the same length of time and there is an Australian Act which has only been law for three or four years. Under law every one of these payments is made to the mother, except when she is judged unfit by someone appointed by the administrating authority. [...]

What will happen if the House allows this proposal to go through unchanged?

The government have decided to leave it to a free vote of the House. I am glad of that, but I would rather they should decide at once, because I realize perfectly well that they have blundered into this decision: it was not a stroke of Machiavellian policy to degrade the status of motherhood.

But the Cabinet is composed of men, and they cannot be expected to realize how women think on this question. I want to warn them of the intensity of women's feelings about it.

They may not all have received many letters, because knowledge of this proposal is only spreading slowly, and no doubt there are quite a number of unimaginative and selfish women who, because their husbands would pay the money to them, are saying: 'What does it matter? It is all right for me.' They should think of their less fortunate sisters.

But the women's organizations are already planning to make sure that every politically conscious woman in the country knows at the next election how her representative has voted.

I took part in that long, bitter struggle for the women's vote before the last war. We did not grudge all that it cost us, because it was worth it, and we got full realization of women's citizenship through it. But I do not want to go through all that again. It was a bitter struggle, and it caused very ugly results.

During these last years, and especially during the war years, women have learned to work together with men, to play together with men, to suffer together with men.

Do we want this sex grievance to raise its ugly head at the next general election, when so many great issues will be before the country; when the whole country ought to be thinking about how the future of the peace of the world ought to be settled by those countries which are now in the bitter throes of war?

Do not force us back into what we thought we had done with – an era of sex antagonism.

If the Bill goes through in its present form I cannot vote for the Third Reading, although I have worked for this thing for over twenty-five years. It would be one of the bitterest disappointments of my political life if the Bill did not go through.

But I foresee too well the consequences if it goes through in a form which practically throws an insult in the faces of those to whom the country owes most, the actual or potential mothers, whom this country needs so badly if we are not to fall into the status of a second-rate Power.

"

JOAN O'CONNELL

'The Promise of a Dream'

TRADES UNION CONGRESS, BLACKPOOL

1968

Joan O'Connell's speech to the Trades Union Congress (TUC) in 1968 is a rousing one. At a key point in the campaign for equal pay, it was a direct emotional and moral challenge to the men in the audience, the trade union movement, employers and the government for their endless inaction. But I also love it because you can hear the reverberations of O'Connell's speech in the ongoing campaign to deliver equal pay in practice today.

At the time, the strike by women machinists at Ford's Dagenham plant had become a powerful symbol of the pay injustice faced by women, and it was still legal to pay women less than men to do the same job. O'Connell was a Dublin member of the Draughtsmen's and Allied Technicians' Association (DATA), active in the Irish trade union movement. She would have been one of only a minority of female delegates at the TUC in Blackpool that year. It was her first time at the TUC and she challenged her fellow trade unionists for failing to do enough, proposing an amendment and calling for action, not just more warm words.

Her speech is punchy and rhythmic, and charged with frustration:

> Barbara Castle has equal pay for equal work; why shouldn't the rest of her sex have it?

Her best lines are in the middle of the speech and I suspect she would have been interrupted by applause. She got a great reception. Newspapers heralded her as 'the toast of the conference', commenting too on her hair, her dress and her voice. Delegates voted for her amendment against the advice of the TUC Council.

Two years after O'Connell gave the speech, and after the Ford Dagenham strike, Labour Cabinet minister Barbara Castle introduced the new Equal Pay Act into Parliament. By 1975, the law had changed.

Delivering equal pay in practice proved harder, and women's pay continued to lag behind that of their male counterparts. But the echoes of the speech could be felt many decades later. When the film and then the musical of *Made in Dagenham* came out many years later, telling the story of the Ford strike, one of the final songs in the musical was a stirring speech from a female trade unionist to the TUC calling on them to support the Dagenham strikers – surely inspired by Joan O'Connell's words. (I have to confess, I saw the musical three times, I enjoyed it so much.)

Soon after the musical opened in London's West End, the cast joined women MPs in Parliament to press for new action from the government to tackle the gender pay gap which still stood at 9.4 per cent.[6] Campaigners seized on the precedent of the Ford strike and used it in speeches in Parliament and beyond to build new support and put pressure on the government. Stronger measures were introduced as a result, requiring employers to publish their gender pay gap, shaming them into action – showing the power of Joan O'Connell's words and the Dagenham women's story to continue helping in the fight for equality today.

"

Our amendment deals with what is undoubtedly the oldest wage claim of the trade union movement - equal pay for equal work.

This claim affects about 8 to 9 million women and has been outstanding for eighty years since the TUC first carried a resolution on equal pay in 1888. Similar resolutions have been carried piously and ad nauseam ever since.

There is nothing more revolting than the annual spectacle at this Congress of women delegates going to the rostrum to beg support from the male members. It has ceased to be funny. The action of the women at Ford's bears this out. They took action as distinct from moralizing about equal pay.

It is fitting in this centenary year to look back over the past eighty years, and one would have to admit that when the history of our great trade union movement is written, one of the less glorious chapters will be that which deals with the regrettable manner in which male members of trade unions have, by their inactivity, condemned all their female members to industrial apartheid which permits the employers of this country to treat women workers as second-class citizens and thereby rob them of some £1,000 million a year.

It is argued that the nation cannot afford this. I say the women workers cannot afford it.

We cannot afford to have 40 per cent of our rightful wages stolen from us. It is high time our trade union movement stopped merely talking about its being unfair. Of course it is unfair and grossly unjust and it will continue until we are prepared to change it by using our industrial strength.

James Connolly once said: 'All workers are slaves, but female workers are the slaves of slaves.' That is as true today as when he said it. […]

Social equality depends on economic equality. If verbal belligerence and moral arguments impressed employers, women would have had equal pay generations ago.

The painful reality is that only 10 per cent of women working in Britain get the same pay as the men they work with. In our opinion, this position will not change until the women of Ford's are joined by thousands of other women workers up and down the country who, by taking industrial action, assert their right to the rate for the job and are supported by the male workers.

For too long the women workers of this country have been fobbed off by pious resolutions, cosy chats and cups of tea in the House of

Commons. Barbara Castle has equal pay for equal work: why should not the rest of her sex have it?

We want more than the promise of a dream.

We have a few women members in D.A.T.A. The majority of those are tracers, but where they are draughtsmen we insist that they are paid the rate for the job. If they are not, we encourage our members to take official action to establish it. We get it then, because this is the only language the employers respect, unfortunate though it is.

Now, after eighty years, is the time for action.

Yesterday Jennie Lee thanked us for making equal pay a live item on the agenda. Well, please don't kill it.

Employers up and down the country who count their profits in millions will be watching this debate anxiously to see whether once again their licence to profiteer on the pathetic wages of women workers will be renewed.

In this centenary year of Congress, what better way of commemorating it than by declaring that the General Council shall call for support for those unions fighting for equal pay?

In supporting this amendment, we ask you to move forward now and give a positive industrial expression to what has for far too long been the mere moral and theoretical position of our trade unions.

AUDRE LORDE

'There Are So Many Silences to Be Broken'

CHICAGO, ILLINOIS

December 1977

More than any other, this speech by Audre Lorde from 1977 sums up the purpose of this book. It is about the impotence of silence and the power of speech – how too often we stay quiet because we fear visibility and the vulnerability that brings, but how we need to find strength in words.

In her own words, Lorde was a 'black, lesbian, mother, warrior, poet' – a champion of the feminist and civil rights movements.[7] Born in 1934 in New York, Lorde worked as a librarian, writer and academic and started publishing her poetry in 1968. Much of her writing was rooted in her personal experience, and she wrote powerfully about identity and the different experiences black women faced, writing in *Sister Outsider*:

> Those of us who stand outside the circle of this society's definition of acceptable women; those of us who have been forged in the crucibles of difference – those of us who are poor, who are lesbians, who are black, who are older – know that survival is not an academic skill. It is learning how to take our differences and make them strengths. For the master's tools will never dismantle the master's house.[8]

This speech in Chicago was given as a short paper to the Modern Languages Association. Lorde had just been through a breast cancer scare. As she reflected on her mortality, she warned 'your silence will not protect you' – and she talks about women bridging their differences to fight together against the shared 'tyranny of silence'.

Most interesting about this speech for me is Lorde's honesty and understanding about how difficult it can be to speak out and the anxiety that comes from exposing your thoughts and words to censure or ridicule. She captures so well the feelings I have often had before making a speech, writing an article or even a tweet – the sense of vulnerability or apprehension that comes from throwing your words out into the world. But she explains how that vulnerability is part of being human, and that we have to share what is most important to us 'even at the risk of having it bruised or misunderstood'.

In part, this speech is a challenge to women to face our fears and speak out, because if we stand by and ignore injustice we will still feel afraid. But Lorde also sees turning silence into words and actions as a personal liberation. For all that Lorde's own words are poetic and quotable, my favourite bit is the quote from her daughter:

You're never really a whole person if you remain silent, because there's always that one little piece inside of you that wants to be spoken out, and if you keep ignoring it, it gets madder and madder and hotter and hotter, and if you don't speak it out one day it will just up and punch you in the mouth.

Lorde and her daughter together speak for all the women in this book who got madder and hotter and bravely broke their silence to inspire others too.

I have come to believe over and over again that what is most important to me must be spoken, made verbal and shared, even at the risk of having it bruised or misunderstood. […]

I am standing here as a black lesbian poet, and the meaning of all that waits upon the fact that I am still alive, and might not have been.

Less than two months ago, I was told by two doctors, one female and one male, that I would have to have breast surgery, and that there was a 60 to 80 per cent chance that the tumour was malignant.

Between the telling and the actual surgery, there was a three-week period of the agony of and involuntary reorganization of my entire life. The surgery was completed, and the growth was benign. But within those three weeks, I was forced to look upon myself and my living with a harsh and urgent clarity that has left me still shaken but much stronger. This is a situation faced by many women, by some of you here today.

Some of what I experienced during that time has helped elucidate for me much of what I feel concerning the transformation of silence into language and action. In becoming forcibly and essentially aware of my own mortality, and of what I wished and wanted for in my life, however short it might be, priorities and omissions became strongly etched in a merciless light and what I most regretted were my silences. […]

I began to recognize a source of power within myself that comes from the knowledge that while it is most desirable not to be afraid, learning to put fear into perspective gave me great strength.

I was going to die, if not sooner then later, whether or not I had ever spoken myself. My silences had not protected me. Your silence will not protect you.

But for every real word spoken, for every attempt I had ever made to speak those truths for which I am still seeking, I had made contact with other women while we examined the words to fit a world in which we all believed, bridging our differences. And it was the concern and caring of all those women which gave me strength and enabled me to scrutinize the essentials of my living.

The women who sustained me through that period were black and white, old and young, lesbian, bisexual and heterosexual, and we all shared a war against the tyrannies of silence. They all gave me a strength and concern without which I could not have survived intact. […]

What are the words you do not have yet? What do you need to say? What are the tyrannies you swallow day by day and attempt to make your own, until you will sicken and die of them, still in silence? Perhaps for some of you here today, I am the face of one of your fears. Because I am a woman, because I am black, because I am myself, a black woman warrior poet doing my work, come to ask you, are you doing yours?

And, of course, I am afraid – you can hear it in my voice – because the transformation of silence into language and action is an act of self-revelation and that always seems fraught with danger.

But my daughter, when I told her of our topic and my difficulty with it, said, 'tell them about how you're never really a whole person if you remain silent, because there's always that one little piece inside of you that wants to be spoken out, and if you keep ignoring it, it gets madder and madder and hotter and hotter, and if you don't speak it out one day it will just up and punch you in the mouth.'

On the cause of silence, each one of us draws her own fear – fear of contempt, of censure, or some judgement, or recognition, of challenge, of annihilation. But most of all, I think, we fear the visibility without which we also cannot truly live.

Within this country where racial difference creates a constant, if unspoken, distortion of vision, black women have on one hand always been highly visible, and so, on the other hand, have been rendered invisible through the depersonalization of racism. Even within the women's movement, we have had to fight, and still do, for that very visibility which also renders us most vulnerable, our blackness.

For to survive in the mouth of this dragon we call America, we have had to learn this first and most vital lesson – that we were never meant to survive. Not as human beings. And neither were most of you here today, black or not.

And that visibility which makes you most vulnerable is also our greatest strength. Because the machine will try to grind us into dust anyway, whether or not we speak. We can sit in our corners mute forever while our sisters and ourselves are wasted, while our children are distorted and destroyed, while our earth is poisoned, we can sit in our safe corners as mute as bottles, and still we will be no less afraid. [...]

In the transformation of silence into language and action, it is vitally necessary to teach by living and speaking those truths which we believe and know beyond understanding. Because in this way alone we can survive, by taking part in a process of life that is creative and continuing, that is growth.

And it is never without fear – of visibility, of the harsh light of scrutiny and perhaps of judgement, of pain, of death. But we have lived through all of those already, in silence, except death. And I remind myself all the time now, that if I was to have been born mute or had maintained an oath of silence my whole life long for safety, I would still have suffered, and I would still die. It is very good for establishing perspective.

And where the words of women are crying to be heard, we must each of us recognize our responsibility to seek those words out, to read them and share them and examine them in their pertinence to our lives. That we not hide behind the mockeries of separations that have been imposed upon us and which so often we accept as our own: for instance, 'I can't possibility teach black women's writing – their experience is so different than mine', yet how many years have you spent teaching Plato and Shakespeare and Proust?

Or another: 'She's a white woman, what could she possibly have to say to me?' Or, 'She's a lesbian, what would my husband say, or my chairman?' Or again, 'This woman writes of her sons and I have no children.' And all the other endless ways in which we rob ourselves of ourselves and each other.

We can learn to work and speak when we are afraid in the same way we have learned to work and speak when we are tired. For we have been socialized to respect fear more than our own needs for language and definition, and while we wait in silence for that final luxury of fearlessness, the weight of that silence will choke us.

The fact that we are here and that I speak these words is an attempt to break that silence and bridge some of those differences between us, for it is not difference which immobilizes us, but silence.

And there are so many silences to be broken.

"

MARGARET THATCHER

'The Lady's Not for Turning'

CONSERVATIVE PARTY CONFERENCE, BRIGHTON

October 1980

When Margaret Thatcher gave this speech to the Conservative Party Conference in the autumn of 1980, she had been Britain's first ever woman prime minister for just eighteen months. Already, she was under fire for her economic policies and her lack of compassion as unemployment had passed 2 million and was still rising.

Her speech could have tried to compensate, could have been defensive, or could have just resorted to party platitudes. But not a bit of it. With the famous line, 'you turn if you want to, the lady's not for turning', Margaret Thatcher set out a defiant, proselytizing and wide-ranging account of her economic and moral philosophy. This is Thatcherism.

For a party conference speech, it is full of serious content, clearly and simply argued. After the obligatory tributes to other cabinet members (not included in this extract), she outlines her faith in monetarism, controlling the money supply and targeting inflation regardless of the consequences for unemployment.

But the real heart of the speech is an ideological assault on the public sector:

> The state drains society, not only of its wealth but of initiative, of energy, the will to improve and innovate as well as to preserve what is best.

Reading her words again now, I want to shout at the page. I think about the teachers who give each next generation the skill as well as the will to innovate, the doctors and nurses who help the sick get their energy back, or the state-funded road builders, construction workers, childcare workers, care workers and police officers who help strengthen our society and help our nation build wealth.

Nine months after this speech was given, I would walk with my dad and the trade union banners in my first political march, aged twelve: the People's March for Jobs. Unemployment would rise to over 3 million. The number of young people in long-term unemployment would soar. In my family and in the coalfield communities I've represented for over twenty years, we were deeply angry at the damage we saw her policies do.

But that's the thing about Margaret Thatcher – she provoked reaction, she didn't build consensus. And she broke the mould. The daughter of a Grantham grocer, she studied chemistry when few women did, then entered politics when it was even more of a boy's club than it is today. It says something about the man's world she was trying to get on in that she took elocution lessons to help lower the pitch of her voice.

Many of her most memorable words were written by others, including her long-time speech writer Sir Ronald Miller who created the 'lady's not for turning' line as a reference to the 1948 Christopher Fry play, *The Lady's Not for Burning*. But wherever those words came from, they capture her. And listening to her self-belief and determination as she uttered them, there is no doubt Margaret Thatcher made them her own.

There are many things to be done to set this nation on the road to recovery, and I do not mean economic recovery alone, but a new independence of spirit and zest for achievement.

It is sometimes said that because of our past, we, as a people, expect too much and set our sights too high. That is not the way I see it. Rather it seems to me that throughout my life in politics our ambitions have steadily shrunk. Our response to disappointment has not been to lengthen our stride but to shorten the distance to be covered. But with confidence in ourselves and in our future, what a nation we could be!

In its first seventeen months, this government have laid the foundations for recovery. We have undertaken a heavy load of legislation, a load we do not intend to repeat because we do not share the socialist fantasy that achievement is measured by the number of laws you pass. [...]

Under Geoffrey [Howe]'s stewardship, Britain has repaid $3,600 million of international debt, debt which had been run up by our predecessors. … Michael Heseltine has given to millions – yes, millions – of council tenants the right to buy their own homes. [...]

The Left continues to refer with relish to the death of capitalism. Well, if this is the death of capitalism, I must say that it is quite a way to go.

But all this will avail us little unless we achieve our prime economic objective – the defeat of inflation. Inflation destroys nations and societies as surely as invading armies do. Inflation is the parent of unemployment. It is the unseen robber of those who have saved. No policy which puts at risk the defeat of inflation – however great its short-term attraction – can be right. [...]

But some people talk as if control of the money supply was a revolutionary policy. Yet it was an essential condition for the recovery of much of continental Europe. Those countries knew what was required for economic stability.

Previously, they had lived through rampant inflation; they knew that it led to suitcase money, massive unemployment and the breakdown of society itself. They determined never to go that way again. Today, after many years of monetary self-discipline, they have stable, prosperous economies better able than ours to withstand the buffeting of world recession. [...]

Meanwhile, we are not heedless of the hardships and worries that accompany the conquest of inflation. Foremost among these is unemployment. Today our country has more than 2 million unemployed. [...]

The level of unemployment in our country today is a human tragedy. Let me make it clear beyond doubt. I am profoundly concerned about unemployment. Human dignity and self-respect are undermined when men and women are condemned to idleness. The waste of a country's most precious assets – the talent and energy of its people – makes it the bounden duty of government to seek a real and lasting cure.

If I could press a button and genuinely solve the unemployment problem, do you think that I would not press that button this instant?

Does anyone imagine that there is the smallest political gain in letting this unemployment continue, or that there is some obscure economic religion which demands this unemployment as part of its ritual?

This government are pursuing the only policy which gives any hope of bringing our people back to real and lasting employment. It is no coincidence that those countries, of which I spoke earlier, which have had lower rates of inflation, have also had lower levels of unemployment.

I know that there is another real worry affecting many of our people. Although they accept that our policies are right, they feel deeply that the burden of carrying them out is falling much more heavily on the private than on the public sector. They say that the public sector is enjoying advantages but the private sector is taking the knocks and at the same time maintaining those in the public sector with better pay and pensions than they enjoy.

I must tell you that I share this concern and understand the resentment. That is why I and my colleagues say that to add to public spending takes away the very money and resources that industry needs to stay in business, let alone to expand. Higher public spending, far from curing unemployment, can be the very vehicle that loses jobs and causes bankruptcies in trade and commerce.

That is why we warned local authorities that since rates are frequently the biggest tax that industry now faces, increases in them can cripple local businesses. Councils must, therefore, learn to cut costs in the same way that companies have to. [...]

If spending money like water was the answer to our country's problems, we would have no problems now. If ever a nation has spent, spent, spent and spent again, ours has.

Today that dream is over. All of that money has got us nowhere, but it still has to come from somewhere.

Those who urge us to relax the squeeze, to spend yet more money indiscriminately in the belief that it will help the unemployed and the small businessman, are not being kind or compassionate or caring. They are not the friends of the unemployed or the small business. They are asking us to do again the very thing that caused the problems in the first place. [...]

It is not the state that creates a healthy society. When the state grows too powerful, people feel that they count for less and less. The state drains society, not only of its wealth but of initiative, of energy, the will to improve and innovate as well as to preserve what is best. Our aim is to let people feel that they count for more and more. If we cannot trust the deepest instincts of our people, we should not be in politics at all. Some aspects of our present society really do offend those instincts.

Decent people do want to do a proper job at work, not to be restrained or intimidated from giving value for money. They believe that honesty should be respected, not derided. They see crime and violence as a threat, not just to society but to their own orderly way of life. They want to be allowed to bring up their children in these beliefs, without the fear that their efforts will be daily frustrated in the name of progress or free expression. Indeed, that is what family life is all about. [...]

A great nation is the voluntary creation of its people – a people composed of men and women whose pride in themselves is founded on the knowledge of what they can give to a community of which they in turn can be proud. If our people feel that they are part of a great nation and they are prepared to will the means to keep it great, a great nation we shall be, and shall remain.

So, what can stop us from achieving this? What then stands in our way? The prospect of another winter of discontent?

I suppose it might. But I prefer to believe that certain lessons have been learned from experience, that we are coming, slowly, painfully, to an autumn of understanding. And I hope that it will be followed by a winter of common sense. If it is not, we shall not be diverted from our course.

To those waiting with bated breath for that favourite media catchphrase, the 'U-turn', I have only one thing to say. 'You turn if you want to. The lady's not for turning.'

MAYA ANGELOU

'On the Pulse of Morning'

INAUGURATION OF PRESIDENT CLINTON, WASHINGTON

January 1993

On a sharp, sunny January morning, I stood in the crowd in front of the US Capitol watching Maya Angelou give this beautiful speech.

It's a poem. But the best speeches are. Written especially for the inauguration of the forty-second president, Bill Clinton, it tells a beautiful story that begins with the enduring river, rock and tree of America's landscape, weaves together people from many nations journeying together from darkness into light, and ends with hope on the pulse of morning, at the start of a brand new day.

Its themes were echoes of those in President Clinton's own inaugural speech, given just a few minutes before – of hope and optimism, of coming together to rebuild.

I'd worked on the Clinton campaign in Arkansas the previous summer. Being the 'man from Hope' was an important part of the Clinton message. But it was Angelou's words, and even more markedly her voice, that I remembered and that truly captured the optimism, warmth and sense of excitement that day. A deep, slow, singing, echoing voice. The poetry itself is beautiful, but it was the emotional power and dignity of its delivery that really made it soar.

Angelou herself had come from silence into words, telling the story in her memoirs of how her rape as a child and the subsequent murder of her rapist had left her traumatized and silenced for many years, but that love of literature and of poetry had brought her voice back.[9]

At the time Angelou summarized the purpose of her poem:

In my work, in everything I do, I mean to say that we human beings are more alike than we are unalike.[10]

This was a message that would be echoed nearly a quarter of a century later in London by the Labour MP Jo Cox in her first parliamentary speech, also included in this collection.

Because while the speech captured a moment of optimism for America in 1992, its real power is in its timelessness as it reminds us that each new hour holds new chances and we should lift up our eyes with hope.

A Rock, A River, A Tree

Hosts to species long since departed,

Marked the mastodon.

The dinosaur, who left dry tokens

Of their sojourn here

On our planet floor,

Any broad alarm of their hastening doom

Is lost in the gloom of dust and ages.

But today, the Rock cries out to us, clearly, forcefully,

Come, you may stand upon my

Back and face your distant destiny,

But seek no haven in my shadow.

I will give you no more hiding place down here.

You, created only a little lower than

The angels, have crouched too long in

The bruising darkness,

Have lain too long

Face down in ignorance.

Your mouths spilling words

Armed for slaughter.

The Rock cries out today, you may stand on me,

But do not hide your face.

Across the wall of the world,

A River sings a beautiful song,

Come rest here by my side.

Each of you a bordered country,

Delicate and strangely made proud,
Yet thrusting perpetually under siege.
Your armed struggles for profit
Have left collars of waste upon
My shore, currents of debris upon my breast.
Yet, today I call you to my riverside,
If you will study war no more. Come,
Clad in peace and I will sing the songs
The Creator gave to me when I and the
Tree and the stone were one.
Before cynicism was a bloody sear across your
Brow and when you yet knew you still
Knew nothing.
The River sings and sings on.
There is a true yearning to respond to
The singing River and the wise Rock.
So say the Asian, the Hispanic, the Jew,
The African and Native American, the Sioux,
The Catholic, the Muslim, the French, the Greek
The Irish, the Rabbi, the Priest, the Sheikh,
The Gay, the Straight, the Preacher,
The privileged, the homeless, the Teacher.
They hear. They all hear
The speaking of the Tree.
Today, the first and last of every Tree
Speaks to humankind. Come to me, here beside the River.
Plant yourself beside me, here beside the River.
Each of you, descendant of some passed
On traveller, has been paid for.

You, who gave me my first name, you
Pawnee, Apache and Seneca, you
Cherokee Nation, who rested with me, then
Forced on bloody feet, left me to the employment of
Other seekers - desperate for gain,
Starving for gold.
You, the Turk, the Swede, the German, the Scot...
You the Ashanti, the Yoruba, the Kru,
Bought, sold, stolen, arriving on a nightmare
Praying for a dream.
Here, root yourselves beside me.
I am the Tree planted by the River,
Which will not be moved.
I, the Rock, I the River, I the Tree
I am yours - your passages have been paid.
Lift up your faces, you have a piercing need
For this bright morning dawning for you.
History, despite its wrenching pain,
Cannot be unlived, and if faced
With courage, need not be lived again.
Lift up your eyes upon
The day breaking for you.
Give birth again
To the dream.
Women, children, men,
Take it into the palms of your hands.
Mold it into the shape of your most
Private need. Sculpt it into
The image of your most public self.

Lift up your hearts
Each new hour holds new chances
For new beginnings.
Do not be wedded forever
To fear, yoked eternally
To brutishness.
The horizon leans forward,
Offering you space to place new steps of change.
Here, on the pulse of this fine day
You may have the courage
To look up and out upon me, the
Rock, the River, the Tree, your country.
No less to Midas than the mendicant.
No less to you now than the mastodon then.
Here on the pulse of this new day
You may have the grace to look up and out
And into your sister's eyes, into
Your brother's face, your country
And say simply
Very simply
With hope
Good morning.

BENAZIR BHUTTO

'The Ethos of Islam Is Equality Between the Sexes'

BEIJING

September 1995

A poem written by Habib Jalib for Benazir Bhutto before she was elected as Pakistan's Prime Minister in 1988 reads:

> *Dartay hain bandooqon aik nihatti larki se.*
> Men with guns fear this unarmed girl.

The men with guns feared Bhutto so much they tried many times to silence her – exiling her, imprisoning her, dismissing her government, threatening her with violence, and eventually assassinating her. But ultimately, they failed to silence her – not just because the words of speeches like this one live on, but also because she inspired future generations of young women in Pakistan and beyond to speak out as she did.

Benazir Bhutto was the first Muslim woman prime minister. In 1990, she became the first premier to give birth while in office; it would be nearly thirty years before New Zealand Prime Minister Jacinda Ardern became the second.

Bhutto was in her twenties when she became the leader of the Pakistan People's Party after her father was executed by the military dictator, General Zia. And she was just thirty-five when she emerged from years of exile, house arrest and prison to win the 1988 elections after Zia died.

In Pakistan's fragile democracy, for a woman to win, promising liberal, social, political and economic reform, was remarkable. But she faced immense internal opposition as right wing and military alliances sought to silence her.

Within a little more than a year of becoming prime minister she became pregnant with her second child. She told no one. After her son was born, she returned straight to work. But it wasn't enough to stop her opponents adding motherhood to the widespread corruption and political charges against her.

This speech was given during her second government at the fourth UN world conference on women held in Beijing in 1995. Hillary Clinton, as First Lady, had already made a strong and often-quoted speech at the conference. Bhutto's speech got less attention, but for women's empowerment it was just as important.

Clinton argued that women's equality is an essential part of the international liberal tradition: 'human rights are women's rights and women's rights are human rights'. Bhutto made a parallel argument that women's equality and empowerment are a central part of Islam: 'the ethos of Islam is equality, equality between the sexes'.

Her speech was, as always, a brave one, challenging social conservatism, Islamist extremism and also international perceptions of Islam. Her rhetoric is strong – repeating her refrain about justice, challenging poverty and insisting that no one should stay neutral in the fight for equality.

Within just over a year of giving this speech, Bhutto was dismissed from government by the President, and shortly afterwards returned to exile. But she didn't give up.

Nearly a decade later, she returned to Pakistan again to campaign for election. Again, she built popular support. But again, she came under attack – particularly the Pakistan Taliban, proponents of the violent Islamist extremism and the oppression of women that Bhutto had challenged. As part of their terrible campaign of fear and destruction, an appalling bomb attack on one of Bhutto's rallies killed 150 people.

Then, on 27 December 2007, at a rally less than two weeks before the election she was expected to win, Benazir Bhutto was assassinated.

The Taliban campaigns failed to silence Bhutto. Eighteen years after Bhutto's UN speech, a fourteen-year-old girl from Pakistan who had also been attacked by the Taliban stood before a UN audience in New York wearing one of Bhutto's shawls and citing Bhutto as an inspiration. Malala Yousafzai spoke powerfully for girls' education and women's empowerment. Her influential words are included in this anthology too.

The Taliban tried to use weapons to silence both Bhutto and Malala. As long as their words keep inspiring new generations of women, the 'men with guns' will not succeed.

As the first woman ever elected to head an Islamic nation, I feel a special responsibility about issues that relate to women.

In addressing the new exigencies of the new century, we must translate dynamic religion into a living reality. We must live by the true spirit of Islam, not only by its rituals.

And for those of you who may be ignorant of Islam, cast aside your preconceptions about the role of women in our religion. Contrary to what many of you may have come to believe, Islam embraces a rich variety of political, social and cultural traditions. The fundamental ethos of Islam is tolerance, dialogue and democracy.

Just as in Christianity and Judaism, we must always be on guard for those who will exploit and manipulate the Holy Book for their own narrow political ends, who will distort the essence of pluralism and tolerance for their own extremist agendas.

To those who claim to speak for Islam but who would deny to women our place in society, I say: the ethos of Islam is equality, equality between the sexes. There is no religion on earth that, in its writing and teachings, is more respectful of the role of women in society than Islam.

My presence here, as the elected woman prime minister of a great Muslim country, is testament to the commitment of Islam to the role of women in society.

It is this tradition of Islam that has empowered me, has strengthened me, has emboldened me.

It was this heritage that sustained me during the most difficult points in my life, for Islam forbids injustice; injustice against people, against nations, against women.

It denounces inequality as the gravest form of injustice.

It enjoins its followers to combat oppression and tyranny.

It enshrines piety as the sole criteria for judging humankind.

It shuns race, colour and gender as a basis of distinction amongst fellow men.

When the human spirit was immersed in the darkness of the Middle Ages, Islam proclaimed equality between men and women. When women were viewed as inferior members of the human family, Islam gave them respect and dignity. When women were treated as chattels, the Prophet of Islam (Peace Be Upon Him) accepted them as equal partners.

Islam codified the rights of women. The Koran elected their status to that of men. It guaranteed their civic, economic and political rights. It recognized their participative role in nation building.

Sadly, the Islamic tenets regarding women were soon discarded. In Islamic society, as in other parts of the world, their rights were denied. Women were maltreated, discriminated against and subjected to violence and oppression, their dignity injured and their role denied.

Women became the victims of a culture of exclusion and male dominance. Today, more women than men suffer from poverty, deprivation and discrimination. Half a billion women are illiterate.

Seventy per cent of the children who are denied elementary education are girls.

The plight of women in the developing countries is unspeakable. Hunger, disease and unremitting toil is their fate. Weak economic growth and inadequate social support systems affect them most seriously and directly. They are the primary victims of structural adjustment processes which necessitate reduced state funding for health, education, medical care and nutrition. Curtailed resource flows to these vital areas impact most severely on the vulnerable groups, particularly women and children.

This, Madam Chairperson, is not acceptable. It offends my religion. It offends my sense of justice and equity. Above all, it offends common sense.

That is why Pakistan, the women of Pakistan, and I personally have been fully engaged in recent international efforts to uphold women's rights. The Universal Declaration of Human Rights enjoins the elimination of discrimination against women. [...]

Women cannot be expected to struggle alone against the forces of discrimination and exploitation. I recall the words of Dante, who reminded us that 'The hottest place in Hell is reserved for those who remain neutral in times of moral crisis' [sic].

Today, in this world, in the fight for the liberation of women, there can be no neutrality.

My spirit carries many a scar of a long and lonely battle against dictatorship and tyranny. I witnessed, at a young age, the overthrow of democracy, the assassination of an elected prime minister, and a systematic assault against the very foundations of a free society.

But our faith in democracy was not broken. The great Pakistani poet and philosopher Dr Allama Iqbal says, 'Tyranny cannot endure forever'. It did not. The will of our people prevailed against the forces of dictatorship. But, my dear sisters, we have learned that democracy alone is not enough. Freedom of choice alone does not guarantee justice. Equal rights are not defined only by political values.

Social justice is a triad of freedom, an equation of liberty: justice is political liberty; justice is economic independence; justice is social equality.

Delegates, sisters, the child who is starving has no human rights. The girl who is illiterate has no future. The woman who cannot plan her life, plan her family, plan a career, is fundamentally not free....

I am determined to change the plight of women in my country. More than 60 million of our women are largely sidelined. It is a personal tragedy for them. It is a national catastrophe for my nation. I am determined to harness their potential to the gigantic task of nation building....

I dream of a Pakistan in which women contribute to their full potential. I am conscious of the struggle that lies ahead. But, with your help, we shall persevere. Allah willing, we shall succeed.

BARBARA CASTLE

'The Red Light Has Gone On'

LABOUR PARTY CONFERENCE, BRIGHTON

September 2000

Barbara Castle was fierce, fabulous and the most significant female Labour politician of the twentieth century. She relished fights and saved lives. And she wasn't afraid to confound people. A non-driver, she brought in the seat belt and the breathalyser as Minister for Transport. A left-winger, she took on the trade unions. A Eurosceptic in the European referendum of 1973, she later became Labour's leader in the European Parliament and called for the party to adopt a more positive approach to Europe in the 1980s. And she made this speech, fierce as ever, a few months before turning ninety.

She grew up in Pontefract, now my constituency – and her politics were heavily influenced by the poverty and hunger she saw during the 1920s miners' strikes. When she crossed the Pennines to be elected for Blackburn in 1945, she was one of only twenty-four women MPs.[11]

And she was a fabulous speaker: commanding, fearless, witty, a twinkle in her eye, robust in her arguments, ready to take anyone on. She should have been Labour's first woman prime minister – and wow, she would have made sparks fly. By the time I met her after she retired many years later, I remember grown Ministers of the Crown still quaking in her wake.

Most famously, she brought in the 1970 Equal Pay Act to make it illegal to pay women less than men. When the female machinists at the Ford factory in Dagenham went on strike, the campaign for equal pay took off. Barbara got involved and helped the machinists obtain a pay rise, but then had to fight to get the rest of the Labour Party and trade union movement to agree to change the law.

I nearly chose her 1969 speech introducing the Equal Pay Bill in Parliament, where she took on the arguments against equal pay with characteristic force and wit:

> We have women working nights on buses, as computer programmers, as air hostesses, in hotels and catering, without giving a second thought to it.

> We women Members would scoff at the idea that we were too frail to do all-night sittings. Indeed, I have noticed that we usually look fresher than the men at the end of them.

But to be honest, despite the historic significance of the speech, most of it doesn't capture Barbara. Too much of it is the worthy outline of legislative clauses, too little of it the wit, passion or polemic she employed on other occasions. Her best speeches are fiercely argumentative – taking on and deconstructing her opponents with humour and ferocity.

In a speech to the Oxford Union during the 1975 referendum, Liberal leader Jeremy Thorpe interrupted her to ask whether her strong opposition to Europe meant that if the country voted 'yes' – to stay in Europe – she would quit as a Cabinet minister. She paused, smiled and retorted, 'If the country votes yes, it will need me to save it.'

There are so many speeches I could have chosen from Barbara, but this one from 2000 captures her fighting spirit, remarkably still going strong at the age of ninety. She was unstoppable – still campaigning and still well aware of how to be the darling of the Conference floor.

Barbara was leading the campaign to get the Labour government to restore the link between pensions and earnings for all pensioners, at a time when Gordon Brown's Cabinet were trying to target help on the poorest.

The speech is short, simple and subversive. Allowed only three minutes to speak in which to persuade people to support her motion against the wishes of Labour ministers, she goes straight for the jugular, specifically challenging the arguments that ministers had made and blowing apart any attempts on their part to try to calm the issue down. The Chair tried to interrupt her as her mere three minutes drew to a close, but didn't stand a chance. This is not Barbara Castle's best oratory, but it's a great testament to the force of her personality.

Thank you, everyone. I have more to say than I have time for.

Comrades, I am sure we were all glad to hear Tony Blair say in ringing tones: 'I am listening, I hear, I will act.'

I could not help wishing that if he had said those words and done those things way back in 1996, when the government, to divert votes from resolutions demanding the earnings link, did not set up the review body. To a man and a woman, all the pensioners on that review body demanded the restoration of the earnings link.

Now they know the financial facts of life, set out so movingly by Alistair Darling - of course they do: they live in the real world as much as we do - yet they cling to the belief that the state insurance scheme is precious and is endangered by the refusal to uprate it each year in line with earnings.

What it means is this. If we continue this policy, the state pension will shrink to about 9 per cent of average earnings by the middle of the next century. To all intents and purposes, it will be dead. I cannot understand it.

The government have listened to all our arguments - they have had to - and I hope that they have listened today. I hope that this resolution will be passed. It is not perfect, but, heavens, unless Conference declares in ringing tones that it wants the restoration of the earnings link, we shall not see it - not in my lifetime anyway.

Alistair Darling's very clever speeches have been telling us how the earnings link would not have done this or that, and people will have more without it. What he fails to tell you is that if Margaret Thatcher had not abolished the earnings link the moment she got into power in 1979, the single state pension today would be worth £97 as of right to everyone. It would have been built up gradually at a bearable cost. I cannot understand why the government are against it. They say they cannot afford it. They admit that the national insurance fund is in surplus and will cover us for the next five years.

A question was asked in the House of Commons recently to which the government's reply was that the surplus was such that by 2010 it would amount to £500 billion. The cost of the earnings link would be £7.5 billion but the revenue would be over £11 billion. That is for the first ten years.

What has been happening to the fund? One of the demands I have made of Gordon Brown is to stop raiding the national insurance fund, which he has been doing, as successive governments have done.

———————————

Chair: Would you start to wind up please.

———————————

Barbara Castle: If they had not been raiding that fund, there would be another £9 billion to pay for pensions.

The red light has gone on. I wish I could have had as much time as Alistair Darling.

Comrades, pass this resolution today; this country can afford it. Remember that the cost of the earnings link rises only when earnings are rising too. Is a wealthy country not going to afford that dignity for all pensioners?

EVA KOR

'A Message of Hope and Healing'

BERLIN

June 2001

This speech by Eva Kor is one of the most important in this anthology. It is hard to find the words to introduce it – hard to think of anything to say that can capture both the unthinkable horror that she endured, but also her remarkable resilience, dignity and optimism.

Eva Kor and her sister Miriam endured the very worst cruelty that humanity could inflict. They were twins, experimented on by Nazi doctor Josef Mengele. Torn from their mother at the gates of Auschwitz, they never saw her again. They were tortured, injected and subjected to experiments – two of the 3,000 Jewish children whom Mengele used and abused as 'human guinea pigs', most of whom were murdered.

Remarkably, Eva and Miriam survived against the odds and after the liberation of Auschwitz they were returned to Romania, then moved to Israel.[12] Half a century later Eva Kor gave this speech to an audience of German doctors in Berlin – describing what happened to her, challenging the medical profession to never again violate human rights and dignity, and speaking about healing.

But the awfulness of what Kor describes is also what makes the second half of her speech so unusual. Mengele himself was never found or brought to justice. But other Nazi doctors were. Kor chose to meet with one of them, to get his public confirmation of the horrors of the Holocaust, and then to forgive him.

Her decision was controversial, many survivors could never have comprehended doing such a thing, but Eva made clear that she did not claim to speak for them nor to forgive on their behalf. Kor said that her forgiveness was not about condoning the atrocities of the Holocaust or excusing Nazi perpetrators, but that it was rather an act of personal healing. As she says in this speech:

I felt a burden of pain was lifted from my shoulders.

It wasn't until the seventies and eighties that Kor and others started to seek out other surviving twins and to speak out – marking the fortieth anniversary of the liberation of Auschwitz with a mock trial for Mengele.

In July 2019, Eva Kor travelled back to Auschwitz as part of the annual educational visit organized by her foundation to help others learn about the horrors of what happened there. It was her last visit. She died while in Poland, aged eighty-five.

As the last of the Holocaust survivors pass away, it feels more important than ever to read and hear their words – in Eva Kor's speech and in others – so that the stories of the Holocaust victims are never forgotten.

Fifty-seven years ago I was a human guinea pig in Auschwitz. ... I am not a spokesperson for all the twins. I am speaking today only for myself. I know that some of my fellow survivors do not share my ideas. But we are all here to be honest, learn the truth and learn from this most tragic chapter of human history. [...]

It was the dawn of an early spring day in 1944 when I arrived in Auschwitz. Our cattle car train came to a sudden stop. I could hear lots of German voices yelling orders outside. We were packed like sardines in the cattle car, and, above the press of bodies, I could see nothing but a small patch of grey sky through the barbed wires on the window. [...]

As soon as we stepped down onto the cement platform, my mother grabbed my twin sister and me by the hand, hoping somehow to protect us. Everything was moving very fast. As I looked around I suddenly realized that my father and two older sisters were gone – I never saw any of them ever again.

As Miriam and I were clutching my mother's hand, an SS hurried by shouting, 'Zwillinge! Zwillinge! Twins – twins?' He stopped to look at my twin sister and me because we were dressed alike and looked very much alike.

'Are they twins?' he asked.

'Is it good?' asked my mother.

'Yes,' nodded the SS.

'Yes, they are twins,' said my mother.

Without any warning or explanation, he grabbed Miriam and me away from Mother. Our screaming and pleading fell on deaf ears. I remember looking back and seeing my mother's arms stretched out in despair as she was pulled in the opposite direction by an SS soldier.

I never got to say 'goodbye' to her and I never got to do so because that was the last time we saw her. All that took thirty minutes. Miriam and I no longer had a family. We were all alone. We did not know what would happen to us. All that was done to us because we were born Jewish. We did not understand why this was a crime. [...]

We were taken to a huge building and were ordered to sit on bleachers, naked, while our clothes were taken away. It was late in the afternoon when our clothes were returned with a big red cross painted on the back. Then our processing began.

When my turn came, I decided that I would not allow them to do to me whatever they wanted, and fought back. When they grabbed my arm to tattoo it, I began to scream, kick and struggle.

Four people – two SS and two women prisoners – restrained me with all their strength, while they heated a pen-like gadget to red hot, then dipped it in ink and burned into my flesh, dot-by-dot, the number capital letter A-7063. [...]

After the evening meal, two girls briefed us about everything in the camp. It was then that we learned about the huge, smoking chimneys and the glowing flames rising high above them. We learned about the two groups of people we had seen on the selection platform and what had happened to them. We learned we were alive only because Dr Mengele wanted to use us in his experiments. […]

Miriam and I went to the latrine at the end of the barrack. There on that filthy floor were the scattered corpses of three children. Their bodies were naked and shrivelled and their wide-open eyes were looking at me. Then and there, I realized that could happen to Miriam and me unless I did something to prevent it. So I made a silent pledge: 'I will do whatever is within my power to make sure that Miriam and I shall not end up on that filthy latrine floor.'

From that moment on, I concentrated all my efforts, all my talents and all my being on one thing: survival. […]

We were starved for food, starved for human kindness and starved for the love of the mothers we once had. We had no rights, but we had a fierce determination to live one more day – to survive one more experiment. … We knew we were there to be subjects of experiments and were totally at the mercy of the Nazi doctors. Our lives depended entirely on the doctors' whims.

Nothing on the face of the earth can prepare a person for a place like Auschwitz. At age ten, I became part of a special group of children who were used as human guinea pigs by Dr Josef Mengele. Some 1,500 sets of multiples were used by Mengele in his deadly experiments. It is estimated that fewer than 200 individuals survived.

In Auschwitz, we lived an emotionally isolated existence. During the whole time I was in Auschwitz, Miriam and I talked very little. All we could say to one another was 'Make sure you don't get sick' and 'Do you have another piece of bread?' It took every ounce of my energy to survive one more day, to live through one more experiment. We did not cry because we knew there was no help. We had learned that within the first few days. [...]

I became very ill after an injection in Mengele's lab. I tried to hide the fact that I was ill because the rumour was that anyone taken to the hospital never came back. The next visit to the lab, they measured my fever and I was taken to the hospital.

The next day a team of Dr Mengele and four other doctors looked at my fever chart and then declared, 'Too bad, she is so young. She has only two weeks to live.'

I was all alone. The doctors I had did not want to heal me. They wanted me dead. Miriam was not with me. I missed her so very much. She was the only kind and loving person I could cuddle up with when I was hungry, cold and scared.

I refused to accept their verdict. I refused to die!

I made a second silent pledge, 'I will do anything in my power to get well and be reunited with my sister, Miriam.' [...]

I was very ill, burning up with fever, between life and death. ... I faded in and out of consciousness. I kept telling myself, 'I must survive. I must survive.'

After two weeks, my fever broke and I began to feel stronger. ... Would I have died, Mengele would have killed Miriam with an injection to the heart and would have done comparative autopsies on our bodies. This is the way most of the twins died. [...]

On a white snowy day, January 27th, 1945, four days before my eleventh birthday, Auschwitz was liberated by the Soviets and we were free. We were alive. We had survived. We had triumphed over unbelievable evil. […]

Those of you who are physicians and scientists are to be congratulated. You have chosen a wonderful and difficult profession; wonderful because you can save human lives and alleviate human suffering but difficult because you are walking a very narrow line.

You have been trained to use good judgement, to be calm, cool and collected, but you cannot forget that you are dealing with human beings. So, make a moral commitment that you will never, ever violate anyone's human rights or take away anyone's human dignity. […]

We are meeting here as former adversaries. I hope we can part as friends.

My people, the Jewish people, are hard-working, intelligent and caring. My people are good people. We did not deserve the treatment we received. No one deserves such treatment.

Your people, the German people, are hard-working, intelligent and caring. … There is a lot of pain that we, the Jewish people, and you, the German people, carry around. It does not help anyone to carry the burden of the past. We must learn to heal ourselves from the tragedies of the Holocaust and help our people to heal their aching souls.

I would like to share with you my ultimate act of healing from the horrors of fifty-six years ago. I do realize that many of my fellow survivors will not share, support or understand my way of healing. There might be some people on both sides who will be angry with me. I understand that. I believe we should not go on suffering forever. This is the way I healed myself. I dare hope that it might work for other people.

I have forgiven the Nazis. I have forgiven everybody. At the fiftieth anniversary observance of the liberation of Auschwitz, in a ceremony attended by my children, … I met with a Nazi doctor, Dr Hans Münch, a former SS doctor at Auschwitz.…

In July, 1993, I received a telephone call from Dr Mihalchick of Boston College who asked me to lecture at a conference on Nazi medicine. Then he added, 'Eva, it would be nice if you could bring a Nazi doctor with you.' I said, 'Dr Mihalchick, where am I going to find a Nazi doctor? The last time I looked they were not advertising in the Yellow Pages.' […]

In 1992, Miriam and I were co-consultants on a documentary on the Mengele Twins done by ZDF, a German television company. In that documentary they had interviewed a Nazi doctor by the name of Dr Hans Münch.

I contacted ZDF to ask them if they would get me Dr Münch's address and phone number, in the memory of my sister who had died the month before. An hour later, I had his address and phone number. … By August, I was on my way to meet Dr Münch. […]

I arrived at Dr Münch's house. I was very nervous. … Dr Münch treated me with the utmost respect. As we sat down to talk, I said to him, 'Here you are – a Nazi doctor from Auschwitz – and here I am – a survivor from Auschwitz – and I like you, and that sounds strange to me.' […]

I asked him if, by any chance, he knew anything about the operation of the gas chambers. And he said, 'This is the nightmare I live with.' Then, he proceeded to tell me about the operation of the gas chambers and that when the bodies were dead, he had signed the death certificates.

I thought about it for a moment, and then I said, 'Dr Münch, I have a big request to make of you. Would you please come with me to Auschwitz in January, 1995, when we will observe fifty years since the liberation of Auschwitz, and sign a document at the ruins of the gas chambers and in the presence of witnesses about what you have told me?' He said yes. I went home delighted that I was going to have a document about the gas chambers at Auschwitz – a document that would help me combat the Revisionists who say that there were no gas chambers.

I tried to think of a way to thank Dr Münch. Then, one day, I thought, 'How about a letter of forgiveness?' I immediately realized that he would like it. I also realized that I had the power to forgive. No one could give me this power and no one could take it away.

I began writing my letter to Dr Münch ... I had no idea what I was doing. I only knew that it made me feel good inside that I had that power. In January, 1995, my children ... and I, and Dr Münch with his children and granddaughter arrived in Auschwitz.

On January 27, 1995, we were standing by the ruins of one of the gas chambers. Dr Münch's document was read and he signed it. I read my Declaration of Amnesty and then signed it. I felt a burden of pain was lifted from my shoulders. I was no longer a victim of Auschwitz. I was no longer a prisoner of my tragic past. I was finally free. So I say to everybody: 'Forgive your worst enemy. It will heal your soul and set you free.'

The day I forgave the Nazis I forgave my parents because they did not save me from a destiny in Auschwitz and I also forgave myself for hating my parents. [...]

How can we build a healthy, peaceful world while all these painful legacies are festering underneath the surface?

I see a world where leaders will advocate and support with legislation the act of forgiveness, amnesty and reconciliation rather than justice and vindictiveness. We have seen in Bosnia, Kosovo and Rwanda, that victims have become victimizers and victimizers have become victims. Let's try something new to end this vicious cycle. [...]

I would like to quote from my Declaration of Amnesty: 'I hope, in some small way, to send the world a message of forgiveness; a message of peace, a message of hope, a message of healing.'

Let there be no more wars, no more experiments without informed consent, no more gas chambers, no more bombs, no more hatred, no more killing, no more Auschwitzes.

THERESA MAY

'Modernizing the Conservative Party'

CONSERVATIVE PARTY CONFERENCE, BOURNEMOUTH

October 2002

Theresa May and I shadowed each other for over twenty years. We were both first elected in 1997, sat together on the same committee (we didn't talk much), were promoted at similar times and ended up opposing each other in senior jobs – first when I was a Labour Cabinet minister, then when she became Conservative Home Secretary. I stood for the leadership of the Labour Party in 2015 and lost. She stood for the leadership of the Conservative Party and position of prime minister in 2016 and won.

We have disagreed a lot over the years, and I have challenged her many times in Parliament on different and difficult issues. I could fill a book with the many things I think she's got wrong and the decisions she's taken that anger me.

But I also respect her as someone who has been a serious and hard-working public servant, who showed sensitivity and judgement when dealing with appalling terrorist attacks that could have divided our country, and also showed remarkable personal resilience throughout her turbulent leadership.

Theresa May was always a strong and authoritative speaker in Parliament, even when under immense pressure. However, her speech to the Conservative Party Conference in 2017 was every politician's worst nightmare; she started coughing and lost her voice, a protester handed her a P45 unemployment slip, and finally the letters literally started to fall off the set behind her. It would have been far-fetched in a TV satire.

There were many contrasting speeches to choose from her parliamentary career. Her words on the steps of Downing Street when first taking office about fighting 'burning injustices' were powerful,[13] although not delivered in practice. Most of her significant speeches as prime minister were on Brexit, including the Lancaster House speech which set red lines to appease her party but also made it harder for her to build consensus in Parliament around a compromise later on.

In the end, however, I have chosen for this book a much earlier speech because I think it was brave. Given to the Tory Party Conference in 2002, much of it is the kind of speech all Conservative Party chairs might give – rallying the faithful, criticizing the Labour Party and so on. But then, suddenly, Theresa May did something different. She took her party on. She challenged them in a thoughtful but robust way over the 'nasty party' image that the Tories had developed.

In the short term, the speech backfired. It reinforced the perception of the party that May was trying to challenge. Labour campaigners could just quote her own words. But in the medium and longer term it was important. It established May as someone who was prepared to do and say difficult things. And it also paved the way for David Cameron's 'modernization' of the Conservative Party which helped them become the largest party in 2010.

She also argued for and worked for more diversity among Tory candidates – including more women candidates and more ethnic minority candidates – and she was one of the first Tories to do so. As a result, by the time she stood down as prime minister, 21 per cent of Conservative MPs were women, compared with 7 per cent when she and I were elected in 1997.[14]

This conference marks a new approach from a party that is changing. Shaping solutions rather than just playing politics. Listening to the people of Britain, who've been so badly let down. Reforming ourselves so that we can reform Britain.

Politics is about public service. Everything we do - in Parliament, in our constituencies, here in Bournemouth - should be motivated by one goal. Improving the lives of our fellow citizens.

At its best, politics is a noble calling. And at their best, politicians - from Churchill to Thatcher - have transformed Britain for the better. But we have to face a deeply uncomfortable truth. One that has been reinforced by what we have been reading in every newspaper over the last two weeks. The public are losing faith in politics.

Politicians are seen as untrustworthy and hypocritical. We talk a different language. We live in a different world. We seem to be scoring points, playing games and seeking personal advantage – while home-owners struggle to make ends meet and schoolchildren see years of hard work undermined by the stroke of a bureaucrat's pen.

Why has the public become so cynical about politics and politicians?

If we're being honest, I think we know the answer. In recent years a number of politicians have behaved disgracefully and then compounded their offences by trying to evade responsibility. We all know who they are. Let's face it, some of them have stood on this platform.

There are many other reasons why voters have learned to disregard what we have to say, however loudly we say it: promising too much and delivering too little; spinning and counter spinning; pursuing our obsessions instead of fighting for the common good.

Fewer and fewer people are bothering to vote. Why? Because they think that politicians will do exactly what they like.

More people vote for a TV show than a political party. And those who do vote think a man dressed as a monkey is more likely to deliver on his election pledges than any party. We might laugh that off. But when they start voting for the BNP then it's time to admit that things have gone badly wrong.

So politicians need to look at themselves. And that, ladies and gentlemen, includes Conservatives.

One of the things that people hate most about modern politics is the almost mindless partisanship that passes for debate. Ya-boo, Punch and Judy, call it what you will, the public is sick of it.

Voters do want the Opposition to scrutinize the government and hold it to account. But voters will only think of the Opposition as an alternative government if the Opposition acts as governments should – in a reasonable way, judging issues on their merits and people on their records. […]

While the parties shout at each other, no one outside the Westminster village pays attention to any of it. People just switch off. British politics has indeed sunk into a rut. […]

Our opponents try to portray our belief in smaller government as not caring about those in need. But this is not, and has never been the case. We reject Labour's 'government knows best' approach, but we certainly don't subscribe to a philosophy that lets people sink or swim.

We believe that an active government should focus on doing what it can to help people get on with their lives. This is the true measure of a compassionate government. And that is why it is imperative that the Conservative Party reforms itself – so that we're in a position to deliver the reforms that most people now accept Britain needs. […]

But the Conservative Party, its principles, its people, have been let down in recent years by the failure of some to represent faithfully the best in Conservatism. Some Tories have tried to make political capital by demonizing minorities instead of showing confidence in all the citizens of our country.

Some Tories have indulged themselves in petty feuding or personal sniping instead of getting behind a leader who is doing an enormous amount to change a party which has suffered two massive landslide defeats. And throughout this week never forget this fact. Twice we went to the country unchanged, unrepentant, just plain unattractive. And twice we got slaughtered. Soldiering on to the next election without radical, fundamental change is simply not an option.

More than that, we must step up the pace of change. […]

But let's not kid ourselves. There's a way to go before we can return to government. There's a lot we need to do in this party of ours. Our base is too narrow and so, occasionally, are our sympathies. You know what some people call us – the nasty party.

I know that's unfair. You know that's unfair, but it's the people out there we need to convince – and we can only do that by avoiding behaviour and attitudes that play into the hands of our opponents. No more glib moralizing, no more hypocritical finger-wagging.

We need to reach out to all areas of our society. I want us to be the party that represents the whole of Britain and not merely some mythical place called 'Middle England', but the truth is that as our country has become more diverse, our party has remained the same.

We should not underestimate the extent of this problem. Ask yourselves: how can we truly claim to be the party of Britain, when we don't truly represent Britain in our party?

Our country is not simply a geographic area. It is the people who live and work in it. It is the people in the inner cities as much as those in the leafy suburbs or rural villages. It's the people in the north and the south, the east and the west. It's the face on the street, whatever its colour, whatever its sex, whatever its background.

Are we really giving everyone in our society a fair chance to represent the Conservative Party?

As a Tory woman I'm instinctively suspicious of positive discrimination. I'm a passionate believer in meritocracy. But are we in the Conservative Party really choosing our candidates on merit? Isn't it time we were more open-minded about what makes the best candidate?

Our associations cherish their independence, but with independence comes responsibility. When selecting a candidate you aren't simply choosing someone to represent your association or your area. Your candidate becomes the face of the Conservative Party. So don't ask yourself whether you would be happy to have a drink with this person on a Sunday morning, ask instead what this person says about us.

At the last general election thirty-eight new Tory MPs were elected. Of that total only one was a woman and none was from an ethnic minority. Is that fair? Is one half of the population entitled to only one place out of thirty-eight?

That's not meritocracy – that's a travesty and it will never be allowed to happen again.

I'm afraid that candidate selection is just one area in which our party seems to many outside our ranks to be hopelessly stuck in the past. The way we look, the way we talk and the way we think – this may be a party at ease with itself, but is it a party at ease with twenty-first-century Britain?

Some people don't like this kind of talk. They say that it's defeatist. Unnecessary. They accuse those of us who raise these concerns of disliking the Conservative Party.

I believe passionately in the Conservative Party. Because I believe passionately that it is the Conservative Party that can make Britain a better society. And it's precisely because I believe passionately in this party of ours that I am utterly determined to see it survive, prosper and win.

Our party is at its best when it takes Conservative principles and applies them to the modern world. It is at its worst when it tries to recreate a bygone age. We cannot bring back the past. We can work together to make today and tomorrow's world a better place.

The values and aspirations that motivate the British people are the same values and aspirations that motivate us. Their priorities are our priorities.

They want better public services first – so do we.

They want to see a society which cares for vulnerable people – so do we.

They want Britain to be better – so do we.

Because we are the party that cares more about where you are going than where you have come from. We are the party for everyone in Britain who wants to change things for the better. The status quo will not do – it's leaving too many people behind. That's why we are committed to change. It's not for its own sake, it's change with a purpose – both in our country and in our party.

We know that the changes we are making to our party will not on their own win us the election. But they will give us a right to be heard. And when our case is heard, it beats our opponents' every time.

Because while they believe in control we believe in freedom.

While they believe in uniformity we believe in choice.

While they trust politicians we trust the people.

And that will always be the difference between us.

History shows us that when the Conservative Party is willing to change, the Conservative Party is ready to win. Our forebears never flinched from modernizing the Conservative Party, so why should we? We exist today because Conservatives of the past understood the need to innovate, to broaden, to be where the people are. Change was our ally and can be so again.

So if you want to live in a society that cares for its vulnerable as much as its strong; if you want to live in a Britain where people are encouraged to grow; if you want to live in a country where hope and opportunity mean something for all – then give us your support.

Play your part. As we focus on rebuilding the Conservative Party into a force that will offer this country a real choice at the next election.

We owe it to ourselves.

We owe it to future generations.

Above all we owe it to Britain.

WANGARI MAATHAI

'A World of Beauty and Wonder'

NOBEL LECTURE, OSLO

December 2004

Wangari Maathai was the first African woman to win a Nobel Peace Prize, and as she accepted it in this speech, she said she hoped it would encourage women and girls 'to raise their voices'.

The speech tells the story of the founding of the Green Belt Movement in the 1970s – how what started as a grassroots campaign to plant trees, protect the environment and prevent poverty grew into a movement for peace and democracy.

Maathai saw how deforestation in Kenya was pushing families into poverty and women were being hardest hit. So she started a movement to plant trees – 50 million of them in Kenya to date – providing jobs for rural women.

The trees started as a way to provide fuel, food, shelter, income, to improve the environment and soil; they became the opportunity for women to gain economic independence and provide education for their children. And then, as the trees and the movement grew, they also became a political symbol for democracy and change. Every tree planted was part of the democratic struggle, every one a symbol of peace.

Maathai was an extremely brave woman. She protested and took legal action against the development of a skyscraper in Kenya's Uhuru Park and won. She went on hunger strike and planted trees with other activists to demand the release of political prisoners and was beaten unconscious by the police. She was even placed on a government list of targets for assassination.

A true trailblazer, Maathai became the first woman in East and Central Africa to gain a PhD, the first to become a professor, the first to win a Nobel Prize.[15] Achim Steiner, director of the UN Environmental Programme, said of her:

> She was, like the acacias and the *Prunus africana* trees Wangari fought so nobly and assiduously to conserve, strong in character and able to survive sometimes the harshest of conditions.[16]

Her speech isn't just a powerful story, it is also a poetic reflection – describing her childhood drinking water straight from a stream, followed by a description of that stream as it is now: dried up. Just as Greta Thunberg would call forty years later for us to recognize our obligations to the next generation, so Maathai challenged us to 'restore the home of the tadpoles and give back to our children a world of beauty and wonder'.

I stand before you and the world humbled by this recognition and uplifted by the honour of being the 2004 Nobel Peace Laureate.

As the first African woman to receive this prize, I accept it on behalf of the people of Kenya and Africa, and indeed the world.

I am especially mindful of women and the girl child. I hope it will encourage them to raise their voices and take more space for leadership. I know the honour also gives a deep sense of pride to our men, both old and young.

As a mother, I appreciate the inspiration this brings to the youth and urge them to use it to pursue their dreams. [...]

My inspiration partly comes from my childhood experiences and observations of nature in rural Kenya. It has been influenced and nurtured by the formal education I was privileged to receive in Kenya, the United States and Germany.

As I was growing up, I witnessed forests being cleared and replaced by commercial plantations, which destroyed local biodiversity and the capacity of the forests to conserve water.

In 1977, when we started the Green Belt Movement, I was partly responding to needs identified by rural women, namely lack of firewood, clean drinking water, balanced diets, shelter and income.

Throughout Africa, women are the primary caretakers, holding significant responsibility for tilling the land and feeding their families.

As a result, they are often the first to become aware of environmental damage as resources become scarce and incapable of sustaining their families.

The women we worked with recounted that, unlike in the past, they were unable to meet their basic needs. This was due to the degradation of their immediate environment as well as the introduction of commercial farming, which replaced the growing of household food crops. But international trade controlled the price of the exports from these small-scale farmers and a reasonable and just income could not be guaranteed.

I came to understand that when the environment is destroyed, plundered or mismanaged, we undermine our quality of life and that of future generations.

Tree planting became a natural choice to address some of the initial basic needs identified by women. Also, tree planting is simple, attainable and guarantees quick, successful results within a reasonable amount of time. This sustains interest and commitment.

So, together, we have planted over 30 million trees that provide fuel, food, shelter, and income to support their children's education and household needs. The activity also creates employment and improves soils and watersheds. Through their involvement, women gain some degree of power over their lives, especially their social and economic position and relevance in the family. This work continues.

Initially, the work was difficult because historically our people have been persuaded to believe that because they are poor, they lack not only capital, but also knowledge and skills to address their challenges. Instead they are conditioned to believe that solutions to their problems must come from 'outside'. Further, women did not realize that meeting their needs depended on their environment being healthy and well managed. [...]

In order to assist communities to understand these linkages, we developed a citizen education program, during which people identify their problems, the causes and possible solutions. ... In the process, the participants discover that they must be part of the solutions. They realize their hidden potential and are empowered to overcome inertia and take action. They come to recognize that they are the primary custodians and beneficiaries of the environment that sustains them. [...]

Although initially the Green Belt Movement's tree-planting activities did not address issues of democracy and peace, it soon became clear that responsible governance of the environment was impossible without democratic space. Therefore, the tree became a symbol for the democratic struggle in Kenya. Citizens were mobilized to challenge widespread abuses of power, corruption and environmental mismanagement. In Nairobi's Uhuru Park, at Freedom Corner, and in many parts of the country, trees of peace were planted to demand the release of prisoners of conscience and a peaceful transition to democracy.

Through the Green Belt Movement, thousands of ordinary citizens were mobilized and empowered to take action and effect change. They learned to overcome fear and a sense of helplessness and moved to defend democratic rights.

In time, the tree also became a symbol for peace and conflict resolution, especially during ethnic conflicts in Kenya when the Green

Belt Movement used peace trees to reconcile disputing communities. During the ongoing rewriting of the Kenyan constitution, similar trees of peace were planted in many parts of the country to promote a culture of peace.

Using trees as a symbol of peace is in keeping with a widespread African tradition. For example, the elders of the Kikuyu carried a staff from the thigi tree that, when placed between two disputing sides, caused them to stop fighting and seek reconciliation. Many communities in Africa have these traditions. [...]

In 2002, the courage, resilience, patience and commitment of members of the Green Belt Movement, other civil society organizations and the Kenyan public culminated in the peaceful transition to a democratic government and laid the foundation for a more stable society.

It is thirty years since we started this work. Activities that devastate the environment and societies continue unabated. Today we are faced with a challenge that calls for a shift in our thinking, so that humanity stops threatening its life-support system.

We are called to assist the earth to heal her wounds and in the process heal our own – indeed, to embrace the whole of creation in all its diversity, beauty and wonder. This will happen if we see the need to revive our sense of belonging to a larger family of life, with which we have shared our evolutionary process.

In the course of history, there comes a time when humanity is called to shift to a new level of consciousness, to reach a higher moral ground. A time when we have to shed our fear and give hope to each other.

That time is now. [...]

As I conclude, I reflect on my childhood experience when I would visit a stream next to our home to fetch water for my mother.

I would drink water straight from the stream. Playing among the arrowroot leaves I tried in vain to pick up the strands of frogs' eggs, believing they were beads. But every time I put my little fingers under them they would break. Later, I saw thousands of tadpoles: black, energetic and wriggling through the clear water against the background of the brown earth. This is the world I inherited from my parents.

Today, over fifty years later, the stream has dried up, women walk long distances for water, which is not always clean, and children will never know what they have lost.

The challenge is to restore the home of the tadpoles and give back to our children a world of beauty and wonder.

ELLEN DEGENERES

'I Know Who I Am'

TULANE UNIVERSITY, NEW ORLEANS

May 2009

Ellen DeGeneres is one of the very few people who is known just by their first name. Everyone knows Ellen. Not everyone knows her story.

Her warm and funny TV chat show is a staple of the American networks – friendly, quirky, positive – while fans from all over the world watch her videos online. My kids have grown up laughing at clips from her shows. Ellen radiates friendliness and I love that she ends every one of her daily talk shows with the phrase 'be kind to one another'.

So it's easy to forget quite how difficult Ellen's journey has been. How the amazing career success she had built up as a comedian and actress by the 1990s was ripped away when she came out as gay. How she coped with the death of a girlfriend when she was young, and the abuse she suffered as a child. How she still found a way from a difficult and dark place to the warmth, fun and positivity her shows exude.

This commencement address to the Tulane graduating class of 2009 in New Orleans tells some of that story – of hitting rock bottom, and then finding a way back.

It's a fun and fabulous speech. It reads as a stream of consciousness. It breaks rules. Almost every sentence begins with 'And'. Jokes and light-heartedness are woven throughout, sometimes popping up as apparently stray thoughts, at apparently inappropriate moments. She makes sentiment more powerful yet less painful by peppering it with smiles.

At the heart of the speech is her description of living with the secret of being gay and of being fearful of the consequences of coming out. Ellen's fears weren't unfounded. After she came out on TV and on the cover of *Time* magazine in 1997 – with the headline 'Yep, I'm Gay' – her sitcom was cancelled by the network and she struggled to find work for several years.

For coming out and speaking out, Ellen paid a considerable personal price. But in doing so, she gave hope and confidence to thousands of LGBT+ people facing their own pressure, fear or discrimination. And the fact that she struggled and rose again, this time to become a national treasure, made her a powerful inspiration in the campaign for LGBT+ equality.

When President Obama awarded Ellen with the Presidential Medal of Freedom in 2016 he remarked on 'how much courage was required for Ellen to come out on the most public of stages'.

There is an added poignancy to the speech in the fact that it was given at Tulane. Ellen grew up in New Orleans. When she gave this commencement speech, the city was still recovering and rebuilding its confidence after the devastation and trauma of Hurricane Katrina a few years before. Her message of warmth to the students, to the city and to herself was, 'You're going to be OK.'

I'm here because I love New Orleans. I was born and raised here, I spent my formative years here, and like you, while I was living here I only did laundry six times. When I finished school, I was completely lost – and by school, I mean middle school, but I went ahead and finished high school anyway. And really, I had no ambition; I didn't know what I wanted to do. I did everything: I shucked oysters, I was a hostess, I was a bartender, I was a waitress, I painted houses, I sold vacuum cleaners; I had no idea and I thought I'd just finally settle in some job and I would make enough money to pay my rent, maybe have basic cable, maybe not, I didn't really have a plan.

My point is that by the time I was your age, I really thought I knew who I was – but I had no idea. Like for example, when I was your age, I was dating men. So what I'm saying is, when you're older, most of you will be gay. Is anybody writing this stuff down? Parents?

Anyway, I had no idea what I wanted to do with my life and the way I ended up on this path was from a very tragic event. I was maybe nineteen, and my girlfriend at the time was killed in a car accident. And

I passed the accident, and I didn't know it was her and I kept going, and I found out shortly after that it was her.

And I was living in a basement apartment; I had no money; I had no heat, no air, I had a mattress on the floor and the apartment was infested with fleas. And I was soul-searching, I was like, why is she suddenly gone, and there are fleas here? I don't understand, there must be a purpose and wouldn't it be so convenient if we could pick up the phone and call God and ask these questions.

And I started writing and what poured out of me was an imaginary conversation with God, which was one-sided, and I finished writing it and I looked at it and I said to myself – and I hadn't even been doing stand-up, ever, there was no club in town – I said, *'I'm going do this on the Tonight Show with Johnny Carson'* (at the time he was the king) *'and I'm going be the first woman in the history of the show to be called over to sit down'.* And several years later, I was the first woman in the history of the show, and only woman in the history of the show, to sit down, because of that phone conversation with God that I wrote.

And I started this path of stand-up and it was successful and it was great but it was hard because I was trying to please everybody and I had this secret that I was keeping, that I was gay. And I thought if people found out they wouldn't like me, they wouldn't laugh at me. Then … I got my own sitcom, and that was very successful, another level of success. And I thought, what if they find out I'm gay, then they'll never watch, and this was a long time ago, this was when we just had white presidents. But anyway, this was back many years ago.

And I finally decided that I was living with so much shame, and so much fear, that I just couldn't live that way anymore and I decided to come out and make it creative. And my character would come out at the same time, and it wasn't to make a political statement, it wasn't to do anything other than to free myself up from this heaviness that I was carrying around, and I just wanted to be honest. And I thought, 'What's the worst that could happen? I can lose my career.' I did. I lost my career. The show was cancelled after six years without even telling me; I read it in the paper. The phone didn't ring for three years. I had no offers. Nobody wanted to touch me at all.

Yet, I was getting letters from kids that almost committed suicide, but didn't because of what I did. And I realized that I had a purpose. And it wasn't just about me and it wasn't about celebrity, but I felt like I was being punished and it was a bad time, I was angry, I was sad, and then I was offered a talk show. And the people that offered me the talk show tried to sell it. And most stations didn't want to pick it up. Most people didn't want to buy it because they thought nobody would watch me.

Really, when I look back on it, I wouldn't change a thing. I mean, it was so important for me to lose everything because I found out what the most important thing is: to be true to yourself. Ultimately, that's what's gotten me to this place. I don't live in fear, I'm free; I have no secrets and I know I'll always be OK, because no matter what, I know who I am.

So, in conclusion, when I was younger I thought success was something different. I thought when I grow up, I want to be famous. I want to be a star. I want to be in movies. When I grow up I want to see the world, drive nice cars, I want to have groupies. To quote the Pussycat Dolls. How many people thought it was 'boobies', by the way? It's not, it's 'groupies'.

But my idea of success is different today. And as you grow, you'll realize the definition of success changes. For many of you, today, success is being able to hold down twenty shots of tequila. For me, the most important thing in your life is to live your life with integrity and not to give in to peer pressure to try to be something that you're not, to live your life as an honest and compassionate person, to contribute in some way. So to conclude my conclusion, follow your passion, stay true to yourself. Never follow anyone else's path, unless you're in the woods and you're lost and you see a path and by all means you should follow that.

Don't give advice, it will come back and bite you in the ass. Don't take anyone's advice. So my advice to you is to be true to yourself and everything will be fine. And I know that a lot of you are concerned about your future, but there's no need to worry. The economy is booming, the job market is wide open, the planet is just fine. It's going be great.

You've already survived a hurricane. What else can happen to you? And as I mentioned before, some of the most devastating things that happen to you will teach you the most. And now you know the right questions to ask in your first job interview. Like, 'Is it above sea level?'

So to conclude my conclusion that I've previously concluded … I guess what I'm trying to say is life is like one big Mardi Gras. But instead of showing your boobs, show people your brain, and if they like what they see, you'll have more beads than you know what to do with and you'll be drunk, most of the time.

So to the Katrina class of 2009, I say congratulations and if you don't remember a thing I said today, remember this, you're going to be OK, dum de dumdumdum, just dance.

ANGELA MERKEL

'A Door Suddenly Opened'

UNITED STATES CONGRESS, WASHINGTON

November 2009

'Tear down walls of ignorance and narrow-mindedness, for nothing has to stay as it is.'

Those were the words of German Chancellor Angela Merkel, not in this 2009 speech made to the US Congress, but in a commencement speech to Harvard University ten years later in 2019.

Having given most of the Harvard speech in German with a translator, for these lines Merkel switched suddenly to address her audience in English. In one simple sentence she invoked the wall Donald Trump wants to build, the wall Germany has taken down, and challenged the walls of prejudice in our minds. She deliberately echoed former US President Ronald Reagan's famous 1987 speech: 'Mr Gorbachev, tear down this wall.'

Merkel's Harvard speech was widely interpreted as a deliberate and determined rejection of the values and world view of American President Donald Trump. But Merkel wasn't just reacting to Trump. Many of the thoughts, images and metaphors in the Harvard 2019 speech had been expressed ten years previously in this speech given to the US Congress in 2009, long before Donald Trump was elected.

Speaking in 2009 to commemorate the twentieth anniversary of the fall of the Berlin Wall, Merkel said:

> We are thus faced with the task of tearing down the walls between different concepts of life ... the walls in people's minds that make it difficult time and again to understand one another.

Both speeches reveal much about the values and vision that have driven Germany's first woman chancellor, its first chancellor from East Germany, its longest-serving chancellor, Europe's longest-serving national leader and one of the most powerful women in the world for the past decade. Both speeches describe her frustration growing up behind the wall that divided a continent and the personal and political liberation she felt once the wall was gone. The later speech is more fluent, more poetic, but I have chosen the earlier one because it feels more important, more prophetic.

This 2009 speech explains so much about some of the most important decisions Merkel would later take. She talks about three things: 'the walls in our minds, the walls of short-sighted self-interest, and the walls between the present and the future'. By which she means prejudice, protectionism and the failure to tackle climate change.

That hostility to the walls that oppress or hold people back would later drive Merkel to offer German sanctuary to hundreds of thousands of Syrian refugees at the height of the Syrian crisis – even though it created a political backlash she had to cope with afterwards.

That hostility to walls and economic barriers between nations also explains Merkel's commitment both to the European project and to economic globalization. But it may also be part of what prevented her and other European governments from doing enough – especially for Greece and Italy during the Eurozone crisis – to help those at the sharp end of globalization.

That hostility to the walls between generations would, in 2015, make her a strong advocate for action to safeguard our planet for the future through the international Paris Agreement on Climate Change.

In the decade between the Congress speech and the Harvard speech, sadly it feels like many of Merkel's walls have grown taller. Far-right extremism and hate crime have risen across Europe and the US, trade barriers are increasing, political divides are deepening, and the Paris Agreement is under threat.

But perhaps the most powerful thing about both speeches is Merkel's faith in change. Her steady optimism. No matter how dark the walls might be, she still believes we can find a door. As she put it in 2009:

> I am convinced that, just as we found the strength in the twentieth century to tear down a wall made of barbed wire and concrete, today we have the strength to overcome the walls of the twenty-first century.

Or as she put it in 2019:

> If we break down the walls that hem us in, if we step out into the open and have the courage to embrace new beginnings, everything is possible.

November 9th is just a few days away. It was on November 9, 1989, that the Berlin Wall fell, and it was also on November 9, in 1938, that an indelible mark was branded into Germany's memory and Europe's history.

On that day the National Socialists destroyed synagogues, setting them on fire, and murdered countless people. It was the beginning of what led to the break with civilization, the Shoah. I cannot stand before you today without remembering the victims of that day and of the Shoah. [...]

It is wonderful that history willed that we should both – the twelve-year-old boy who was driven out of Germany [Professor Fritz Stern] and me, the Chancellor of a reunited Germany who was born in the GDR – be here in this distinguished House. This fills me with great joy and deep gratitude.

Not even in my wildest dreams could I have imagined, twenty years ago before the Wall fell, that this would happen. It was beyond imagination then to even think about travelling to the United States of America let alone standing here today.

The land of unlimited opportunity – for a long time it was impossible for me to reach. The Wall, barbed wire and the order to shoot those who tried to leave, limited my access to the free world. So I had to create my own picture of the United States from films and books, some of which were smuggled in from the West by relatives. What did I see and what did I read? What was I passionate about?

I was passionate about the American dream – the opportunity for everyone to be successful, to make it in life through their own personal effort. I, like many other teenagers, was passionate about a certain brand of jeans that were not available in the GDR and which my aunt in West Germany regularly sent to me. […]

On November 9, 1989, the Berlin Wall came down. The border that for decades had divided a nation into two worlds was now open. And that is why, for me, today is, first of all, the time to say thank you. […]

I know, we Germans know, how much we owe to you, our American friends. … All over Europe the common quest for freedom released an incredible power: in the trade union Solidarność in Poland, amongst the reformers surrounding Václav Havel in Czechoslovakia, at the first opening of the Iron Curtain in Hungary and at the demonstrations that took place every Monday in the GDR.

Where there was once only a dark wall, a door suddenly opened and we all walked through it: onto the streets, into the churches, across the borders. Everyone was given the chance to build something new, to make a difference, to venture a new beginning.

I also started anew. I left my job as a physicist at the Academy of Sciences in East Berlin behind me and went into politics. Because I finally had the chance to make a difference. Because I had the impression that now it was possible to change things. It was possible for me to do something.

Twenty years have passed since we were given this incredible gift of freedom. But there is still nothing that inspires me more, nothing that spurs me on more, nothing that fills me more with positive feelings than the power of freedom.

A person who has experienced such a positive surprise in life believes that much is possible. Or, to put it in the words of Bill Clinton in Berlin in 1994: 'Nothing will stop us. All things are possible.' […]

All things are possible, also in the twenty-first century, in the age of globalization. We back home in Germany know just as well as you do in America that many people are afraid of globalization.

We do not just brush these concerns aside. We recognize the difficulties. And yet it is our duty to convince people that globalization is an immense global opportunity, for each and every continent, because it forces us to act together with others.

The alternative to globalization would be shutting ourselves off from others, but this is not a viable alternative. It would lead only to isolation and therefore misery. […]

Ladies and gentlemen, it is true that America and Europe have had their share of disagreements. One may feel the other is sometimes too hesitant and fearful, or from the opposite perspective, too headstrong and pushy. And nevertheless, I am deeply convinced that there is no better partner for Europe than America and no better partner for America than Europe.

Because what brings Europeans and Americans together and keeps them together is not just a shared history. What brings and keeps Europeans and Americans together are not just shared interests and the common global challenges that all regions of the world face. That alone would not be sufficient to explain the very special partnership between Europe and America and make it last.

It is more than that. That which brings Europeans and Americans closer together and keeps them close is a common basis of shared values. It is a common idea of the individual and his inviolable dignity. It is a common understanding of freedom in responsibility. This is what we stand for in the unique transatlantic partnership and in the community of shared values that is NATO. […]

This basis of values was what ended the Cold War, and it is this basis of values that will enable us to stand the tests of our times – and these tests we must stand.

Germany is united, Europe is united. That is what we have achieved. Now, today, our political generation must prove that it is able to meet the challenges of the twenty-first century, and that in a sense it is able to tear down today's walls.

What does that mean? First it means building peace and security, second, achieving prosperity and justice, and third, protecting our planet. […]

Even after the end of the Cold War we are thus faced with the task of tearing down the walls between different concepts of life, in other words the walls in people's minds that make it difficult time and again to understand one another in this world of ours.

This is why the ability to show tolerance is so important. ... There are different ways to create peaceful coexistence. Tolerance means showing respect for other people's history, traditions, religion and cultural identity.

But let there be no misunderstanding: tolerance does not mean 'anything goes'. There must be zero tolerance towards all those who show no respect for the inalienable rights of the individual and who violate human rights. [...]

Freedom is the very essence of our economy and society. Without freedom the human mind is prevented from unleashing its creative force. But what is also clear is that this freedom does not stand alone. It is freedom in responsibility and freedom to exercise responsibility. For that reason the world needs order. The near collapse of the international financial markets showed what happens when there is no such order.

If there is one lesson the world has learned from last year's financial crisis, it is that there is no alternative to a global framework for a globalized economy. [...]

In a way this is a second wall that has to fall: a wall standing in the way of a truly global economic order, a wall of regional and exclusively national thinking. [...]

This crisis was also an expression of too much short-term thinking. Millions of people all over the world might lose their jobs or even suffer poverty and starvation because of this. To achieve prosperity and justice we must do all we can to prevent such a crisis in the future. [...]

The fact that global challenges can only be met by comprehensive international cooperation is also shown by a third great challenge of the twenty-first century, by a wall, so to speak, separating the present from the future. That wall prevents us from seeing the needs of future generations, it prevents us from taking the measures urgently needed to protect the very basis of our life and climate.

We can already see where this wasteful attitude towards our future leads: in the Arctic icebergs are melting, in Africa people are becoming refugees due to environmental damage, and global sea levels are rising. […]

I am convinced that, just as we found the strength in the twentieth century to tear down a wall made of barbed wire and concrete, today we have the strength to overcome the walls of the twenty-first century, walls in our minds, walls of short-sighted self-interest, walls between the present and the future.

ALISON DRAKE

'Get Up There and Get At It'

CASTLEFORD

September 2010

I spent a long time trying to find a recording or a transcript of one of the many speeches made by Alison Drake, a brilliant Yorkshire community activist, and a close friend of mine for many years.

Born and bred in Castleford, Alison was a former teacher in my constituency who had been forced to retire after a debilitating accident. She had a tough time of it, but she fought back, becoming a tireless advocate for our community. She was incredibly proud of our town and its history – from its Roman roots, to the coal industry, to Henry Moore. But she also knew that community pride was crucial to building confidence in the future too. She wanted Castleford children to be proud of where they came from so that they would have the confidence to do amazing things.

Like the woman herself, Alison's speeches were brilliant. She speaks for millions of women who say what they think, who fight for their communities, and whose words never get written down or heard outside their towns. Back in the late nineties and early noughties, Alison and I would often make speeches together at community events. We were trying to get new investment in Castleford after years of decline since the pits closed, and we'd managed to get several of our local towns included in a government-funded regeneration programme. We were determined it would be community led, so the local council leader and I chaired a series of public meetings which hundreds of local people came along to, putting ideas forward and volunteering to get involved.

When Alison spoke, she could shape the whole mood and direction of a meeting. She would talk about the hardship people faced, and the industry and jobs we had lost. But she would also tell a story to be proud of, usually rooted in some wonderful part of Castleford's history, its working-class communities or a quirky corner of our town. We all learned early not to resist an Alison request because she was bound to get her way eventually. But she did everything in a coaxing, persuasive way – simultaneously charming international architects and chivvying friends and neighbours to work together in the interests of our town.

At Alison's urging, the town has rediscovered its historic connection to its waterways, turning back towards the river again, and thanks to her persistence we now have an internationally renowned new curving bridge across the River Aire.

The Castleford Heritage Group she founded (and made me president of) has taken over the old flour mill on the riverbank. Retired builders, millworkers, engineers, carpenters and managers from across the area have been mobilized to help regenerate it bit by bit. We now have a cafe, an exhibition space, a Yorkshire craft beer shop and a boat house – all run by local people.

I haven't managed to find one of Alison's most rousing early speeches, as none of us recorded them or wrote them down. But that doesn't mean they have been lost or forgotten – those words started something important for our community. To reflect that, I have managed to find a recording of Alison speaking many years later about the work we all did – and that's what I've included here.

Alison died while I was putting this anthology together. In Castleford, we miss her still. But she has left us an incredible legacy, and I want her voice to be remembered too.

I'm proud of the last ten years of what we've achieved in Castleford.

When we started out, the town had had fifteen years trying to recover from the miners' strike, the loss of all our mining industries and the local industries that had been important in the past: the chemicals, the glass works and the pottery works, brick-making and confectionery, clothing. But most of them have gone now. Trying to recover from all that loss was horrendous, and as we hit the millennium we wanted something better.

People got together in big meetings where 400 people would turn up to have their say. We wanted something better and we really worked for that. We're a close-knit community. There might be 40,000 people in this town, but everybody knows everybody. We put notices up around the town and put it in the local press that if you wanted a say on the future of Castleford and you wanted something better for our town – come along. And they did and they continued to do so.

Different groups were formed. All kinds of different groups: community groups, residence groups, friends of the park, friends of the library, the Heritage Trust. They were all forming at the end of the nineties and in 2000, because we had got to the stage where we felt something was happening nationally with the new government and because of the spirit of the new age as a result of the new millennium.

We put together a strategy with the help of the council, where we were designing projects for the town centre that could improve the image and then the local environment around the town. ... Local people know our towns best. We've got three fantastic local councillors for the town centre totally on our side because they're local people. And that fight wasn't hard, except when it came to the district level because of course Castleford wasn't on their radar in terms of regeneration.

We put together a strategy. Getting it delivered wasn't going to be quick or easy and what made the difference for us between succeeding and having to wait twenty-five years was Yorkshire Forward, the Regional Development Agency, the active local councillors and our MP Yvette Cooper who was in the Cabinet by that time – and the local people pushing all that together, making Wakefield [Council] sit up and take notice.

What we've got to do is keep it up, motivating new people to get involved, because lots of young people out there haven't been involved over the last ten years and can't remember the heritage we're talking about – that we value all the pits and the pit sites. It's long gone to them. We want them to feel part of what we're doing now, so they own the present but also own the past and understand their roots and understand where older people like myself are coming from.

So just get up there and get at it.

"

MARIE COLVIN

'Someone Has To Go There'

LONDON

November 2010

It is hard to do justice to Marie Colvin in a few short words. As foreign correspondent for the *Sunday Times* for over twenty years, Colvin travelled to the places others fled – reporting from Chechnya, Libya, Kosovo, Sri Lanka, Syria and Iraq. Time and again she put her own life at risk to tell the stories of those whose lives, families and countries were being destroyed by war. In 2010, she gave this deeply personal and poignant speech at a memorial service for journalists killed in conflict, reflecting on the risks, traumas and purpose of working as a war correspondent. Looking back at it now, the speech reads as a haunting valedictory. Less than two years later, as one of the only international reporters left in the besieged Syrian city of Homs, she lost her own life when the makeshift media centre she was working from was hit by Syrian government rockets.

Fellow foreign correspondent, friend, and latterly Colvin's biographer, Lindsey Hilsum describes her as the journalist who always 'went further and stayed longer'. Few of us can imagine being so courageous. Her journalism was always compelling and her bravery helped save lives. In Fallujah, Iraq, she hired a digger to uncover a mass grave of murdered Kuwaiti prisoners of war. Her refusal to leave East Timor in 1999, and the articles she wrote as Indonesian-backed forces advanced on a refugee compound of 1,500 Timorese women and children, pressured UN officials into staying and helped to prevent a massacre.

Those who knew her describe her as a remarkable combination of strength and compassion – charismatic, driven, funny, stylish, hard-living, hard-drinking. She bore deep emotional and physical scars: post-traumatic stress, recurrent nightmares and a patch over her right eye that became her trademark after losing the eye in a grenade attack in Sri Lanka.

Colvin talks about that attack and the loss of her eye in the speech. Standing in the serene and beautiful St Bride's Church in London – known across the world as 'the journalists' church' as it is just off Fleet Street, the old beating heart of the newspaper industry – she describes the fear and terror of stepping through landmine-infested territory in Afghanistan, constantly questioning whether the dangers faced were worth it, and addresses the fine line between bravery and bravado. Knowing as we do what was to happen in Syria soon after, it is hard not to feel a deep unease as she talks about a newspaper headline that ran 'Has Marie Colvin gone too far this time?' – and her definitive answer, 'It is worth it.'

Ultimately, Colvin's speech is a determined, almost defiant, account of the importance of war reporting, 'to bear witness ...

trying to find the truth in a sandstorm of propaganda' – a truth about the brutal destruction and human trauma of war that she argues you cannot fully uncover unless someone goes there to see it first hand. As she put it in an article after she lost her eye, 'I am not going to hang up my flak jacket as a result of this incident ... I'll be more awed than ever by the quiet bravery of civilians who endure far more than I ever will. They must stay where they are. I can come home.'

I wanted to include Colvin's speech not just because of her own bravery, and her dedication to exposing the brutal reality behind conflict, but also because her speech and articles give wider testimony to the importance of seeking and championing truth. At a time when the very notion of truth feels under constant siege – from populist politics, 'fake news', 'alternative facts' and a casual dismissal of experts – it feels more important than ever to recognize and honour those who dedicate their lives and careers to uncovering and protecting the truth, and through this protecting our democratic values.

At the time of writing, the Committee to Protect Journalists estimates that 824 journalists have been killed in conflict zones around the world in the last decade; they have been murdered, caught up in crossfire or died on dangerous assignments. Like Marie Colvin, they are worthy of the medals of war heroes, and they too must never be forgotten.

Your Royal Highness, ladies and gentlemen, I am honoured and humbled to be speaking to you at this service tonight to remember the journalists and their support staff who gave their lives to report from the war zones of the twenty-first century. I have been a war correspondent for most of my professional life. It has always been a hard calling. But the need for frontline, objective reporting has never been more compelling.

Covering a war means going to places torn by chaos, destruction and death, and trying to bear witness. It means trying to find the truth in a sandstorm of propaganda when armies, tribes or terrorists clash. And yes, it means taking risks, not just for yourself but often for the people who work closely with you.

Despite all the videos you see from the Ministry of Defence or the Pentagon, and all the sanitized language describing smart bombs and pinpoint strikes, the scene on the ground has remained remarkably the same for hundreds of years. Craters. Burned houses. Mutilated bodies. Women weeping for children and husbands. Men for their wives, mothers, children. Our mission is to report these horrors of war with accuracy and without prejudice. We always have to ask ourselves whether the level of risk is worth the story. What is bravery, and what is bravado?

Journalists covering combat shoulder great responsibilities and face difficult choices. Sometimes they pay the ultimate price. Tonight we honour the forty-nine journalists and support staff who were killed

---

bringing the news to our shores. We also remember journalists around the world who have been wounded, maimed or kidnapped and held hostage for months. It has never been more dangerous to be a war correspondent, because the journalist in the combat zone has become a prime target.

I lost my eye in an ambush in the Sri Lankan civil war. I had gone to the northern Tamil area from which journalists were banned, and found an unreported humanitarian disaster. As I was smuggled back across the internal border a soldier launched a grenade at me and the shrapnel sliced into my face and chest. He knew what he was doing.

Just last week, I had a coffee in Afghanistan with a photographer friend, Joao Silva. We talked about the terror one feels, and must contain, when patrolling on an embed with the armed forces through fields and villages in Afghanistan … putting one foot in front of the other, steeling yourself each step for the blast. The expectation of that blast is the stuff of nightmares. Two days after our meeting, Joao stepped on a mine and lost both legs at the knee.

Many of you here must have asked yourselves, or be asking yourselves now, is it worth the cost in lives, heartbreak, loss? Can we really make a difference? I faced that question when I was injured. In fact one paper ran a headline saying, 'Has Marie Colvin gone too far this time?' My answer then, and now, was that it is worth it. Today in this church are friends, colleagues and families who know exactly what I am talking about, and bear the cost of those experiences, as do their families and loved ones.

Today we must also remember how important it is that news organizations continue to invest in sending us out at great cost, both financial and emotional, to cover stories. We go to remote war zones to report what is happening. The public have a right to know what our government, and our armed forces, are doing in our name. Our mission is to speak the truth to power. We send home that first rough draft of history. We can and do make a difference in exposing the horrors of war and especially the atrocities that befall civilians. […]

War reporting has changed greatly in just the last few years. Now we go to war with a satellite phone, laptop, video camera and a flak jacket. I point my satellite phone to south-south-west in Afghanistan, press a button and I have filed.

In an age of 24/7 rolling news, blogs and Twitter, we are on constant call wherever we are. But war reporting is still essentially the same – someone has to go there and see what is happening. You can't get that information without going to places where people are being shot at, and others are shooting at you. The real difficulty is having enough faith in humanity to believe that enough people – be they government, military or the man on the street – will care when your file reaches the printed page, the website or the TV screen.

We do have that faith because we believe we do make a difference. And we could not make that difference – or begin to do our job – without the fixers, drivers and translators who face the same risks and die in appalling numbers. Today we honour them as much as the frontline journalists who have died in pursuit of the truth. They have kept the faith as we who remain must continue to do.

99

Marie Colvin

JOANNE O'RIORDAN

'No Limbs No Limits'

'GIRLS IN TECHNOLOGY' CONFERENCE, NEW YORK

April 2012

When Joanne O'Riordan gave this speech to the International Telecommunication Union conference on Girls in Technology she was just sixteen years old. She has an extremely rare condition known as Total Amelia, meaning she has no limbs. This speech is an incredible account of how she never lets it hold her back.

O'Riordan is a sports journalist for the *Irish Times* with a degree in criminology, and is a long standing campaigner for disability rights. In a Cork TEDx Talk in the same year as this speech, she described how the combination of technology and determination 'has allowed me to live a life that has astonished people beyond belief ... I do things in my life that any other able-bodied person can do with their limbs.'

In theory this New York speech is about technology. She describes some of the practical things it has helped her do and the independence it has given her. It is an exciting account of the potential of robotics, computing and new waves of research to empower everyone, to address disability and make amazing new things possible.

In practice the speech is about indomitable humanity. At its heart is O'Riordan's own determination and creativity – her refusal to be held back, her family's support and her enthusiasm for trying new things, solving new problems and overcoming impossible challenges. Her optimism is infectious and she uses it to encourage others to be determined and creative too.

The speech has a clear structure and message – telling her personal story, championing technology and urging girls to build robots. But throughout it all, her real message is the inspiration to everyone to challenge and overcome their own limits, building up to a great final line:

> Just because I have no limbs does not mean I will be limited.
> And neither should you!

Good afternoon everyone! My name is Joanne O'Riordan and firstly I'd like to thank all of those at the United Nations and the people from the International Telecommunication Union for this amazing and unique opportunity to speak here in front of you today.

Being invited to New York the week of my sixteenth birthday is simply unbelievable.

As you can see, I was born without my limbs, but my motto in life is 'No Limbs No Limits'.

The disability I have is known as Total Amelia and it is one of the rarest conditions known to us. I believe there are only seven people in the world living with this physical form and furthermore there is no medical explanation as to why I was born this way.

However, my family and I have never allowed it to hold me back. From an early age I have always relied on the use of technology to help advance my abilities. Be this in moving or communicating, I developed an understanding of what I could achieve with technology from a young age.

I use technology in all aspects of my life, be it at home, in school or through the wider medium of interacting with others. My parents have told me that when I was one I first began to explore the use of technology with our old computer. I figured out how to use this software by simply moving my 'hand' and chin at a faster speed. Today I can type thirty-six words a minute, and for someone with no limbs, I think that's an incredible achievement in itself.

The computer allowed me to play and follow certain games, which in turn helped me to learn my ABCs, maths and small words such as 'cat' and 'dog'. Needless to say, I'm a fiercely independent person, but when I was born the technology that was there then was not as advanced as the technology we have now.

All my young life I've struggled and overcome barriers. I've surprised doctors, strangers, friends and even my own family by what I have achieved. I must admit I'm always finding new ways or methods that would allow me to be the same as any other person. There is no such thing as 'normal' in my vocabulary.

When I started school I, like all the other children, used my hand to write. I did this by putting my pen in between my shoulder and chin, and as you can imagine this was an enormous challenge for me, but I overcame the obstacle.

I have always been breaking down barriers and overcoming obstacles. I do not look at the word 'Impossible' and see it as 'Impossible'. I look at that word and my life and say, 'I'm Possible'!

Technology has made me even more determined to achieve a better standard and quality of life. I always think, if I can do this now, what would I achieve in the future? Technology, as we know, is ever advancing and my question was soon answered when, at the age of seven, I started to develop a spinal condition known as scoliosis. This is a curvature of the spine. Unfortunately, this meant that I was not able to continue to write as I did, and I had to find a new way of learning and developing my educational potential.

I'm very lucky that I have the support of my family, as they have never allowed anyone to hold me back. They have done everything in their power to ensure that I would not lose out on my education, and technology was key in helping me.

A system was set up which allows my schoolbooks to be put on to CD. This in turn enables me to do all my work through a computer. ... I can use my mobile phone, send texts, tweets, update my Facebook, play my PlayStation, Nintendo DS, iPad, iPod and laptop; without Microsoft, Adobe and Apple in my life I would not be doing and achieving my full potential. In fact, I think my life would be quite different to what it is now. Believe it or not I simply use my upper and bottom lip, chin, nose and hand to work most, if not all, of these systems.

Technology has opened up a world of possibilities, through which I have excelled in both my education and social environment around me. It is fair to say that I have been given the opportunities to grow, learn and adapt my lifestyle in a way that helps me, but I also know there are children and adults out there all over the world who do not have the same chances in life as I do.

I'm asking the Girls in Technology who are here today and who are the leading women within their field to start doing what I do, in my life: 'Think outside the box.'

Think of ways and means that you can make technology more accessible to those who really need it, because let's face it, we all know women are better than men at most things, so why not technology too?

It is my wish and it's my challenge to you and to others out there to build me a robot. Yes, that's right, a robot! It sounds almost insane, but as a child and even today I've always wanted and would love to have a robot. […]

Call it crazy, call it insane, call it what you like – but the challenges I face every day get bigger and far greater to overcome. I know I can overcome these challenges but I need your help. I can't rely on my parents, my brothers, sister and others all my life. Can I? Certainly not, and I don't want to!

I want to live an independent life, just like you. I don't want to live in the shadow of others because I want to make my own journey in life, and I know if I'm given that chance I can and will succeed. I know that there must be someone out there in the world who can do something like this to make life much easier. It would not just help me, but indeed others who are in similar situations.

Life is about living and let's face it ladies, technology is not just a way of life, it's a way of living! And just because I have no limbs does not mean I will be limited. And neither should you!

"

MANAL
AL-SHARIF

'Driving for Freedom'

OSLO FREEDOM FORUM

May 2012

In May 2011, Manal al-Sharif got into her brother's car and drove through the Saudi city of Khobar. She asked a friend to film her driving and then posted it on YouTube, then she asked other women to do the same. Within twenty-four hours al-Sharif had been arrested and imprisoned. Her offence? Being a woman behind the wheel in Saudi Arabia.

The protests she inspired that summer set the country on a slow course towards easing some of the most restrictive measures against women. But with many women activists still in exile or in prison, their struggles are far from over. This speech, given in Oslo a year after that first YouTube post, is al-Sharif's story of what happened and of her own awakening; it is a fierce cry for the freedom for which she and other brave Saudi women continue to fight.

Al-Sharif founded the Women2Drive movement in the wake of the Arab Spring, to protest not just the taboo against women driving, but the Saudi male guardianship system that required women to seek the permission of their father, brother, husband or even son before they could travel, work, access healthcare, marry, obtain a passport or make many other personal decisions. As she describes in the speech, 'the struggle is not about driving a car, the struggle is about being in the driver's seat of our own destiny, about being free not just to dream but free to live'.

Those protests in the summer of 2011 broke the taboo against women driving. They helped to give Saudi women confidence and provoked a national debate and an international wave of support for al-Sharif and others. Inch by inch, things started to change, until in the autumn of 2017 the Crown Prince announced he was granting women the right to drive in the Kingdom of Saudi Arabia. Licences were to be issued from 2018, alongside the gradual introduction of other reforms allowing women to travel, work, play sport and apply for their own passports.[17]

But the apparent victory came at a cost. Since the very first protests in 2011, al-Sharif has been targeted by threats, calls for her to be publicly flogged, smears and character assassinations, and has been forced to move abroad. Driven from her job as a computer scientist by the backlash, driven from her marriage and home by domestic abuse, she described a few years later how 'without a safe place to work or live, with other Saudis calling for my death, I had no choice but to leave the only country I had ever known'.[18]

Saudi custody laws meant she had to leave her oldest son behind, and Saudi marriage and visa laws mean she cannot return with her younger son, born in her second marriage.[19]

Many of al-Sharif's fellow campaigners have endured similar persecution and just weeks before the 2018 change in the law several women were arrested. Amnesty International has recorded how they have been beaten, tortured and subjected to sexual assault. Some, like Loujain al-Hathloul, are still in prison without trial.[20] Al-Sharif, who had planned to come back to her homeland and drive from coast to coast to mark the change in the law, was deterred from doing so for fear that she, too, would be detained. The apparent success of the campaign has been undermined by the silencing of its champions. Women who put themselves at risk to campaign for an end to male guardianship laws are still not free.

Manal al-Sharif continues to speak out and campaign for women's rights and human rights in Saudi Arabia. Even from abroad, such action demands great bravery – especially since the brutal assassination of Saudi journalist Jamal Khashoggi in Turkey in 2018. She has achieved so much on her personal journey, from growing up fearful and ashamed of being a woman to becoming an international champion of women's rights across the world. Laws in her home country have slowly started to change and many other women have been empowered to become activists as a result. But it is the knowledge of all that has happened since this 2012 speech, and how far things still have to go, that gives poignancy to the pause in her closing remarks: 'The struggle will end, but I am not sure when.'

As women, we were raised to listen, follow, and never ask why. If you don't follow the rules, we were taught that we would burn in hellfire in our grave and in the afterlife. Many nights I spent in tears, trying to do all I could to please God, to follow the rules. I thought it would have been much easier to just die, because living with these rules was simply impossible.

As a woman I was taught that if I left home I would be fully responsible for any evil that happened, because men can't control their instincts. I am the seductive fruit, they said, and I would seduce men in all my shapes and forms. So, my place should be home. I was taught that as a woman I am only Awra (sinful to expose). My face was Awra, my voice was Awra, even my name was Awra. I started covering fully, top to toe in black, when I was ten years old. […]

We were faceless, voiceless and nameless. We were the invisible women.

I was just eleven when the news broke all over the country that forty-seven women had challenged the ban on women driving in Riyadh. The announcer on TV announced days later that, according to the recent fatwa of Sheikh Bin Baz, the Grand Mufti of Saudi Arabia, women driving was haram – forbidden in Islam. The Ministry of Interior warned everyone that women were not allowed to drive in the Kingdom of Saudi Arabia. Horrible rumours were spreading about those forty-seven women, and they were called awful names. We, as kids, had been told those women were bad and we should never be like them. For the next twenty-two years, talking about this subject was banned.

Another taboo was created: Women Driving. […]

We were inspired by the Arab Spring, and we were led by personal struggle; we were a group of Saudi women who, realizing that there was no law to ban us from driving, started the Women2Drive campaign.

One night I was leaving my doctor's clinic in Al-Khobar at 9 p.m., and I couldn't find a ride back home. A car kept chasing me, and I was almost kidnapped. The next day at work I was horrified and angry, and I complained to my colleague how it's frustrating that I have a driver's licence but I'm not allowed to drive, just because I'm a woman. He broke the good/bad news to my face: 'But there is no law banning you from driving.'

That ignited the whole idea in my mind of starting a campaign to call women to get behind the wheel and drive on 17 June 2011. We encouraged women with international driver's licences only to participate, as we didn't want accidents that day. We started a Facebook page, followed by a Twitter account and a seven-minute video I recorded using my webcam; I posted it on YouTube to explain who we are and the idea behind 17 June.

I showed my face, I spoke with my voice, I used my real name. For me, the time of fear and silence was over. I used to be ashamed of who I am – a woman. But not any more. I was there to speak up for myself.

Later that month, I recorded a video of myself driving in the city of Khobar and posted it on YouTube. It got 700,000 views on the first day. A day later I was arrested for driving and sent to jail for nine days.

Newspapers and TV were closely following my story - it broke a huge riot around the country; it became a hot topic at every house and every gathering place. Calls to send me to a trial were roaring. There were even calls to flog me in a public place, to make me an example to other women.

I was called all names in the book for that simple act: whore, outcast, licentious, immoral, rebellious, disobedient, Iran agenda, Westernized, traitor, double agent, etc. Rumours of all kinds spread everywhere. The hardest thing wasn't facing what I did, it was facing what I didn't do.

On 17 June the streets were packed with police cars and religious police SUVs to scare anyone who thought to drive that day. Despite all that pressure, some hundred women broke the ban and drove on 17 June. None were arrested. We broke the taboo.

On 15 November 2011, I filed the first lawsuit against the Saudi General Directorate of Traffic in the administrative court for not issuing me a driver's licence.

We can talk freely now in the media and newspapers about women driving. Women themselves are not the same anymore. We united for the first time, the previous generation and this generation. We are using positive pressure to push for change. We are called now 'My Right to Dignity', calling for full citizenship for Saudi women, ending decades of male guardianship. [...]

A year later, the same newspapers that cracked down on me harshly are publishing the news of my international honouring and awards. My mother shed many tears facing all kind of attacks on her daughter. I called her that day when the local newspaper that was the worst in attacking me finally published a small article about me with the title 'Manal is a role model for Saudi women'. The article came after announcing my name amongst the *Time* 100 most influential people in the world. I told my mother, 'Here is your rehabilitation.' Mum had tears that day, but a different kind of tears for the first time in a year; they were the tears of pride and joy.

I always tell my mother, 'They might handcuff me and send me behind jail bars, but I will never accept them putting cuffs on my mind. They can break my bones, Mum, but they can never break my soul.'

Years of being passive, whispering complaints with so many years of signing petitions and waiting for a response that would never come, we decided finally that the time of silence is over. We took action to change our reality. Waiting will result in nothing but more waiting and frustration. But, sadly, even a year later, women are still waiting for a miracle to happen to change their reality; they are still waiting for a royal decree to lift the ban on women driving. They don't know it will never come to them. It's up to them to take the key and go behind the wheel and just drive, as simple as it sounds, as simple as it is.

I believe that children cannot be free if their mothers are not free, parents cannot be free if their daughters are not free, husbands cannot be free if their wives cannot be free. Society is nothing, if women are nothing.

For me, freedom starts within. Here [in my heart] I know I am free, but there, in Saudi, I am certain the struggle has just began. The struggle will end, but I am not sure when. The struggle is not about driving a car, the struggle is about being in the driver's seat of our own destiny, about being free not just to dream but free to live.

JULIA GILLARD

'He Needs a Mirror'

AUSTRALIAN PARLIAMENT, CANBERRA

October 2012

Five months before Australian Prime Minister Julia Gillard made this speech in the Australian Parliament, I met her briefly on a visit to Canberra.

I had been frankly flabbergasted by the full-frontal misogyny she was facing as prime minister. This wasn't coming from the margins, it was mainstream – headed up by the Leader of the Opposition, Tony Abbott.

Gillard had become Australia's first woman prime minister in 2010. Politics was fraught with a hung Parliament, a controversial carbon tax and ongoing divisions within the Labor Party. Nevertheless, the campaign against Gillard's government became highly charged, hugely personalized and shot through with sexism – often attacking her for being unmarried and childless.

Abbott stood with campaigners in front of placards saying 'Ditch the witch' and 'Julia … Bob Brown's Bitch'. On another occasion an Opposition fundraising dinner menu included 'Julia Gillard Quail' – 'small breasts, huge thighs and a big red box'.[21]

This was still a few years before the rise of misogynistic abuse towards Hillary Clinton in the US or the keyboard warrior explosion of sexism and abuse towards women in public life took off in the UK. But viral emails and newly emerging Facebook groups encouraging sexualized and violent abuse towards Gillard had started to spread.

Then, in October 2012, Abbott opened a debate in Parliament attacking Gillard for failing to sack the Labor Speaker, the Member for Fisher, Peter Slipper, over crude and sexist texts he had sent. Gillard's response in this speech is nothing short of a controlled explosion. It's worth watching as well as reading. The words on the page are sharp, but they are nothing compared with seeing Gillard take down Abbott to his face – barely looking at her notes, pelting him from across the floor with example after example of his sexism.

Her fury is more powerful for being controlled. Her argument is more powerful for being forensic. She had a long, detailed list of charges to put forward. Abbott – forced to listen to it – became visibly more and more uncomfortable. In the following weeks, Gillard's speech accumulated millions of views online. Back in Westminster I cheered watching it. Gillard spoke for millions of women who are sick and tired of putting up with insidious sexism and double standards. Less than a year of turbulent Australian politics later, including considerable Labor infighting, Gillard stood down. In her final speech as prime minister eight months later, referring to the sexism she'd faced, she said:

> It doesn't explain everything, it doesn't explain nothing, it explains some things. ... It will be easier for the next woman and the woman after that and the woman after that. And I'm proud of that.[22]

"

Thank you very much Deputy Speaker and I rise to oppose the motion moved by the Leader of the Opposition. And in so doing I say to the Leader of the Opposition I will not be lectured about sexism and misogyny by this man.

I will not. And the government will not be lectured about sexism and misogyny by this man. Not now, not ever.

The Leader of the Opposition says that people who hold sexist views and who are misogynists are not appropriate for high office. Well I hope the Leader of the Opposition has got a piece of paper and he is writing out his resignation.

Because if he wants to know what misogyny looks like in modern Australia, he doesn't need a motion in the House of Representatives, he needs a mirror. That's what he needs.

Let's go through the Opposition Leader's repulsive double standards, repulsive double standards when it comes to misogyny and sexism. We are now supposed to take seriously that the Leader of the Opposition is offended by Mr Slipper's text messages, when this is the Leader of the Opposition who has said, and this was when he was a minister under the last government – not when he was a student, not when he was in high school – when he was a minister under the last government.

He has said, and I quote, in a discussion about women being under-represented in institutions of power in Australia … the Leader of the Opposition says, 'If it's true, Stavros [the interviewer], that men have more power generally speaking than women, is that a bad thing?'

And then a discussion ensues, and another person being interviewed says, 'I want my daughter to have as much opportunity as my son.' To which the Leader of the Opposition says, 'Yeah, I completely agree, but what if men are by physiology or temperament, more adapted to exercise authority or to issue command?'

Then ensues another discussion about women's role in modern society, and the other person participating in the discussion says, 'I think it's very hard to deny that there is an under-representation of women,' to which the Leader of the Opposition says, 'But now, there's an assumption that this is a bad thing.'

This is the man from whom we're supposed to take lectures about sexism.

And then of course it goes on. I was very offended, personally, when the Leader of the Opposition, as Minister of Health, said, and I quote, 'Abortion is the easy way out.' I was very personally offended by those comments. You said that in March 2004, I suggest you check the records.

I was also very offended on behalf of the women of Australia when in the course of this carbon pricing campaign, the Leader of the Opposition said, 'What the housewives of Australia need to understand as they do the ironing...'

Thank you for that painting of women's roles in modern Australia.

And then of course, I was offended too by the sexism, by the misogyny, of the Leader of the Opposition catcalling across this table at me as I sit here as prime minister, 'If the Prime Minister wants to, politically speaking, make an honest woman of herself...' – something that would never have been said to any man sitting in this chair.

I was offended when the Leader of the Opposition went outside the front of Parliament and stood next to a sign that said 'Ditch the witch'.

I was offended when the Leader of the Opposition stood next to a sign that described me as a man's bitch.

I was offended by those things.

Misogyny, sexism, every day from this Leader of the Opposition.

Every day in every way, across the time the Leader of the Opposition has sat in that chair and I've sat in this chair, that is all we have heard from him.

And now, the Leader of the Opposition wants to be taken seriously, apparently he's woken up after this track record and all of these statements, he's woken up and he's gone, 'Oh dear, there's this thing called sexism, oh my lords, there's this thing called misogyny. Now who's one of them? Oh, the Speaker must be because that suits my political purpose.'

Doesn't turn a hair about any of his past statements, doesn't walk into this Parliament and apologize to the women of Australia. Doesn't walk into this Parliament and apologize to me for the things that have come out of his mouth. But now seeks to use this as a battering ram against someone else.

Well this kind of hypocrisy should not be tolerated, which is why this motion from the Leader of the Opposition should not be taken seriously. […]

The Leader of the Opposition and the Deputy Leader of the Opposition have come into this place and have talked about the Member for Fisher. Well, let me remind the Opposition and the Leader of the Opposition particularly about their track record and association with the Member for Fisher. […]

I remind the Leader of the Opposition, who now comes in here and speaks about apparently his inability to work with or talk to Mr Slipper. I remind the Leader of the Opposition, he attended Mr Slipper's wedding.

Did he walk up to Mr Slipper in the middle of the service and say he was disgusted to be there? Was that the attitude he took? No, he attended that wedding as a friend.

The Leader of the Opposition is keen to lecture others about what they ought to know or did know about Mr Slipper. Well with respect, I'd say to the Leader of the Opposition, after a long personal association, including attending Mr Slipper's wedding, it would be interesting to know whether the Leader of the Opposition was surprised by these text messages. He's certainly in a position to speak more intimately about Mr Slipper than I am, and many other people in this Parliament, given this long personal association. […]

On the conduct of Mr Slipper, and on the text messages that are in the public domain, I have seen the press reports of those text messages. I am offended by their content. I am offended by their content because I am always offended by sexism. I am offended by their content because I am always offended by statements that are anti-women. […]

I also believe, in terms of this Parliament making a decision about the speakership, that this Parliament should recognize that there is a court case in progress. That the judge has reserved his decision, that having waited for a number of months for the legal matters surrounding Mr Slipper to come to a conclusion, that this Parliament should see that conclusion.

I believe that is the appropriate path forward, and that people will then have an opportunity to make up their minds with the fullest information available to them. But whenever people make up their minds about those questions, what I won't stand for, what I will never stand for, is the Leader of the Opposition coming into this place and peddling a double standard. […]

Peddling a standard for Mr Slipper that has not been acquitted by the people who have been sent out to say the vilest and most revolting things, like his former Shadow Parliamentary Secretary, Senator Bernardi.

I will not ever see the Leader of the Opposition seek to impose his double standard on this Parliament. Sexism should always be unacceptable. … The Leader of the Opposition says do something; well he could do something himself if he wants to deal with sexism in this Parliament.

He could change his behaviour, he could apologize for all his past statements, he could apologize for standing next to signs describing me as a witch and a bitch, terminology that is now objected to by the frontbench of the Opposition. He could change a standard himself if he sought to do so. But we will see none of that from the Leader of the Opposition because on these questions he is incapable of change. Capable of double standards, but incapable of change.

His double standards should not rule this Parliament. Good sense, common sense, proper process is what should rule this Parliament. That's what I believe is the path forward for this Parliament, not the kind of double standards and political game-playing imposed by the Leader of the Opposition now looking at his watch because apparently a woman's spoken too long.

I've had him yell at me to shut up in the past, but I will take the remaining seconds of my speaking time to say to the Leader of the Opposition I think the best course for him is to reflect on the standards he's exhibited in public life, on the responsibility he should take for his public statements, on his close personal connection with Peter Slipper, on the hypocrisy he has displayed in this House today.

And on that basis, because of the Leader of the Opposition's motivations, this Parliament today should reject this motion and the Leader of the Opposition should think seriously about the role of women in public life and in Australian society because we are entitled to a better standard than this.

CHIMAMANDA NGOZI ADICHIE

'We Should All Be Feminists'

TED TALK, LONDON

April 2013

Chimamanda Ngozi Adichie's speech 'We Should All Be Feminists' is full of joy and humour, and wonderful personal stories of growing up a feminist in Nigeria. Given as a TEDx Talk, it has reached over 3.5 million people online. Published as a book it has been a success across the world. Beyoncé sampled the speech in her song 'Flawless'. A Swedish project has gifted the book to every sixteen-year-old in the country.

This isn't Adichie's only TED Talk. Her speech 'The Danger of a

Single Story' has become one of the most watched TED Talks of all time[23] – challenging the under-representation of different cultures and our readiness to judge people, communities and nations based only on one story we know about them.

TED Talks are the perfect format for Adichie's witty and thought-provoking speeches. They have transformed the oral tradition, providing new ways to reach millions of people online with an interesting argument – shorter and more entertaining than academic lectures or formal addresses, more relaxed and wide-ranging than political rallies. There are great TED Talks to watch on an amazing range of topics, but Adichie's particularly stand out.

Adichie's power as a speaker comes in part from her strengths as a novelist and storyteller. Her words are beautiful and she makes them come alive with evocative vignettes, often from her own experiences. The gender inequality and injustice Adichie describes in her speech comes across powerfully because she roots it in the everyday experiences of relatable characters – often friends and family.

These personal stories make the speech far more compelling, but they also allow her to weave in complexity and nuance about gender inequality – so she can get across clear ideas but without being overly simplistic or getting trapped in the single story she warns us against.

But the beauty of her speeches is also in the performance. In this TED Talk, Adichie's delivery is warm, with great timing and a twinkle in her eye. And it is also optimistic and inclusive, arguing that women and men both benefit when 'freer to be our true individual selves' without the weight of gender expectations. Ultimately, the power of this speech is that it makes feminism not just a plea for a fairer world but a call for a happier, more joyous world.

I wrote a novel about a man who, among other things, beats his wife and whose story doesn't end very well. When I was promoting the novel in Nigeria, a journalist, a nice, well-meaning man, told me he wanted to advise me. And to the Nigerians here, I'm sure we're all familiar with how quick our people are to give unsolicited advice.

He told me that people were saying that my novel was feminist and his advice to me – and he was shaking his head sadly as he spoke – was that I should never call myself a feminist because feminists are women who are unhappy because they cannot find husbands.

So I decided to call myself a 'happy feminist'.

Then, an academic, a Nigerian woman, told me that feminism was not our culture, that feminism wasn't Africa, and that I was calling myself a feminist because I had been corrupted by 'Western' books, which amused me because a lot of my early [Western] reading was decidedly un-feminist. […]

But anyway, since feminism was un-African, I decided I would now call myself a happy African feminist. At some point I was a happy African feminist who does not hate men and who likes lip gloss and who wears high heels for herself but not for men.

Of course, a lot of this was tongue-in-cheek, but that word 'feminist' is so heavy with baggage, negative baggage. […]

Now, here's a story from my childhood. When I was in primary school, my teacher said at the beginning of term that she would give the class a test, and whoever got the highest score would be the class monitor.

Now, class monitor was a big deal. If you were a class monitor, you got to write down the names of noise-makers, which was heady enough power on its own. But my teacher would also give you a cane to hold in your hand while you walked around and patrolled the class for noise-makers. Now, of course you were not actually allowed to use the cane, but it was an exciting prospect for the nine-year-old me.

I very much wanted to be the class monitor, and I got the highest score on the test. Then to my surprise my teacher said that the monitor had to be a boy. She had forgotten to make that clear earlier because she assumed it was obvious. […]

I often make the mistake of thinking that something that is obvious to me is just as obvious to everyone else.

Now take my dear friend Louis, for example. Louis is a brilliant, progressive man and we would have conversations and he would tell me, 'I don't know what you mean by things being different or harder for women. Maybe in the past, but not now.' And I didn't understand how Louis could not see what seemed so self-evident.

Then one evening in Lagos, Louis and I went out with friends. And for people here who are familiar with Lagos, there's that wonderful Lagos fixture, the sprinkling of energetic men who hang around outside establishments and very dramatically help you park your car.

I was impressed with the particular theatrics of the man who found us a parking spot that evening. And so as we were leaving, I decided to leave him a tip.

I opened my bag, put my hand inside my bag, brought out my money that I had earned from doing my work, and I gave it to the man. And he, this man who was very grateful and very happy, took the money from me, looked across at Louis, and said, 'Thank you, sir!'

Louis looked at me surprised, and asked, 'Why is he thanking me? I didn't give him the money.' Then I saw realization dawn on Louis's face. The man believed that whatever money I had had ultimately come from Louis, because Louis is a man.

Now, men and women are different.

We have different hormones, we have different sexual organs, we have different biological abilities; women can have babies, men can't, at least not yet. Men have testosterone, and are in general physically stronger than women. There are slightly more women than men in the world, about 52 per cent of the world's population is female. But most of the positions of power and prestige are occupied by men.

The late Kenyan Nobel Peace Laureate, Wangari Maathai, put it simply and well when she said, 'The higher you go the fewer women there are.' […]

And this made sense a thousand years ago. Because human beings lived then in a world in which physical strength was the most important attribute for survival. The physically stronger person was more likely to lead. […]

But today we live in a vastly different world. The person more likely to lead is not the physically stronger person, it is the more creative person, the more intelligent person, the more innovative person, and there are no hormones for those attributes. […]

Some weeks ago I walked into the lobby of one of the best Nigerian hotels. … And a guy at the entrance stopped me and asked me annoying questions. Because the automatic assumption is that a Nigerian female walking into a hotel alone is a sex worker. […]

Each time I walk into a Nigerian restaurant with a man, the waiter greets the man and ignores me. […]

Each time they ignore me, I feel invisible. […]

Gender matters everywhere in the world, but I want to focus on Nigeria, and on Africa in general, because it is where I know and because it is where my heart is.

And I would like today to ask that we begin to dream about and plan for a different world. A fairer world. A world of happier men and happier women who are truer to themselves.

And this is how to start. We must raise our daughters differently. We must also raise our sons differently. We do a great disservice to boys in how we raise them. We stifle the humanity of boys. We define masculinity in a very narrow way. Masculinity becomes this hard, small cage and we put boys inside the cage. We teach boys to be afraid of fear. We teach boys to be afraid of weakness, of vulnerability. We teach them to mask their true selves because they have to be, in Nigeria speak, 'hard man'. […]

The more 'hard man' a man feels compelled to be, the weaker his ego is. And then we do a much greater disservice to girls because we raise them to cater to the fragile egos of men.

We teach girls to shrink themselves, to make themselves smaller. We say to girls, 'You can have ambition, but not too much. You should aim to be successful, but not too successful, otherwise you would threaten the man. If you are the bread winner in your relationship with a man, you have to pretend that you're not. Especially in public. Otherwise you will emasculate him.' […]

Because I am female, I am expected to aspire to marriage. I am expected to make my life choices always keeping in mind that marriage is the most important. […]

I know a woman who decided to sell her house because she didn't want to intimidate a man who might marry her. I know an unmarried woman in Nigeria who, when she goes to conferences, wears a wedding ring, because according to her, she wants all the participants in the conference to give her respect. I know young women who are under so much pressure from family, from friends, even from work to get married, and they're pushed to make terrible choices. […]

Both men and women in Nigeria will say – and this is an expression I am very amused by – 'I did it for peace in my marriage'. Now, when men say it, it is usually about something that they should not be doing anyway … 'Oh, my wife said I can't go to the club every night, so for peace in my marriage I do it only on weekends.' Now, when a woman says, 'I did it for peace in my marriage', she is usually talking about having given up a job, a dream, a career. […]

We teach girls that they cannot be sexual beings in the way that boys are. […]

But of course, when the time is right, we expect those girls to bring back the perfect man to be their husbands. We police girls. We praise girls for virginity, but we don't praise boys for virginity. And it's always made me wonder how exactly this is all supposed to work out... [applause] I mean, the loss of virginity is usually a process that involves two people. […]

We teach girls shame. 'Close your legs. Cover yourself.' We make them feel as though by being born female they're already guilty of something. And so, girls grow up to be women who cannot say they have desire. They grow up to be women who silence themselves. They grow up to be women who cannot say what they truly think. […]

The problem with gender is that it prescribes how we should be rather than recognizing how we are. Now, imagine how much happier we would be, how much freer to be our true individual selves, if we didn't have the weight of gender expectations. […]

I have chosen to no longer be apologetic for my femaleness and for my femininity. And I want to be respected in all of my femaleness because I deserve to be. […]

Gender matters. Men and women experience the world differently. Gender colours the way we experience the world.

But we can change that. […]

Some people will say that a woman being subordinate to a man is our culture. But culture is constantly changing. I have beautiful twin nieces who are fifteen who live in Lagos. If they had been born 100 years ago, they would have been taken away and killed because it was our culture, it was the Ibo/Igbo culture to kill twins. […]

Culture does not make people. People make culture. […]

My own definition of feminist is: a feminist is a man or a woman who says, 'Yes, there's a problem with gender as it is today, and we must fix it, we must do better.'

MALALA YOUSAFZAI

'Let Us Pick Up Our Books and Our Pens'

UN GENERAL ASSEMBLY, NEW YORK

July 2013

On her sixteenth birthday, nine months after being shot in the head by the Taliban, Malala Yousafzai gave a speech to the United Nations. A teenage figure on the world stage, honoured to be wearing Benazir Bhutto's pale pink shawl, she spoke slowly and clearly about her experience.

Nothing changed in my life except this: weakness, fear and hopelessness died. Strength, power and courage was born. I am the same Malala. My ambitions are the same. My hopes are the same. And my dreams are the same.

The speech had a huge impact on everyone who heard it, and for me, with teenagers of my own at the time, I could only imagine the changes in her life since the previous year, from the moment when a Taliban gunman asked the group of Pashtun schoolgirls at the back of the Khushal school bus, 'Who is Malala?', and then shot her and her friends at close range. And then on this day in July 2013 – less than a year later – making her first public address at the United Nations.

But personal loss and suffering was not her message. Her rallying cry for education was so powerful because she'd almost been killed in her pursuit of it. But in this speech she subverts the violent imagery of weapons and turns it on its head – it is the extremists who should be afraid because we have the most powerful weapon of all.

Let us empower ourselves with the weapon of knowledge ...
let us pick up our books and our pens.

Malala has described Benazir Bhutto as one of her inspirations, and when Ban Ki-moon introduced Malala to the youth assembly that day, he echoed the words Habib Jalib had written for Bhutto many years before, that those with guns feared an unarmed girl: 'By targeting Malala, extremists showed what they feared the most: a girl with a book.'

And he was right. Malala's speech and her tireless campaigning for girls' education since then has been the most defiant riposte to the Taliban brutality that had failed to silence her.

She ends with rhetoric and timing worthy of a seasoned campaigner calling upon world leaders, governments, developed nations, communities and sisters across the world to unite for the cause of education.

One child, one teacher, one book and one pen can change the world.

Since then, Malala has won a Nobel Peace Prize, and with her family set up the Malala Fund, supporting activists who work for girls' education in Afghanistan, Brazil, India, Nigeria and Pakistan.

Today it is an honour for me to be speaking again after a long time. Being here with such honourable people is a great moment in my life and it is an honour for me that today I am wearing a shawl of Benazir Bhutto Shahid. […]

Today is the day of every woman, every boy and every girl who have raised their voice for their rights. There are hundreds of human rights activists and social workers who are not only speaking for their rights, but who are struggling to achieve their goal of peace, education and equality.

Thousands of people have been killed by the terrorists and millions have been injured. I am just one of them. So here I stand, one girl among many. I speak not for myself, but for those without a voice can be heard. Those who have fought for their rights. Their right to live in peace. Their right to be treated with dignity. Their right to equality of opportunity. Their right to be educated.

Dear friends, on 9 October 2012, the Taliban shot me on the left side of my forehead. They shot my friends, too. They thought that the bullets would silence us, but they failed. And out of that silence came thousands of voices.

The terrorists thought they would change my aims and stop my ambitions. But nothing changed in my life except this: weakness, fear and hopelessness died. Strength, power and courage was born. I am the same Malala. My ambitions are the same. My hopes are the same. And my dreams are the same.

Dear sisters and brothers, I am not against anyone. Neither am I here to speak in terms of personal revenge against the Taliban or any other terrorist group. I am here to speak up for the right of education for every child. I want education for the sons and daughters of the Taliban and all the terrorists and extremists. I do not even hate the Talib who shot me.

Even if there is a gun in my hand and he stands in front of me, I would not shoot him. This is the compassion that I have learned from Muhammad, the prophet of mercy, and Jesus Christ and Lord Buddha. This is the legacy of change that I have inherited from Martin Luther King, Nelson Mandela and Muhammad Ali Jinnah.

This is the philosophy of non-violence that I have learned from Gandhi Jee, Bacha Khan and Mother Teresa. And this is the forgiveness that I have learned from my father and from my mother.

This is what my soul is telling me: be peaceful and love everyone.

Dear sisters and brothers, we realize the importance of light when we see darkness. We realize the importance of our voice when we are silenced. In the same way, when we were in Swat, the north of Pakistan, we realized the importance of pens and books when we saw the guns. The wise saying, 'The pen is mightier than the sword', was true.

The extremists were – and they are – afraid of books and pens. The power of education frightens them. They are afraid of women. The power of the voice of women frightens them.

And that is why they killed fourteen innocent students in the recent attack in Quetta. And that is why they killed female teachers.… That is why they are blasting schools every day because they were and they are afraid of change, afraid of equality that we will bring to our society.

And I remember that there was a boy in our school who was asked by a journalist: 'Why are the Taliban against education?' He answered very simply by pointing to his book, he said: 'A Talib doesn't know what is written inside this book.'

They think that God is a tiny, little conservative being who would send girls to the hell just for going to school. The terrorists are misusing the name of Islam and Pashtun society for their own personal benefits. Pakistan is a peace-loving, democratic country. Pashtuns want education for their daughters and sons.

And Islam is a religion of peace, humanity and brotherhood. Islam says that it is not only each child's right to get education, rather it is their duty and responsibility. Peace is necessary for education. In many parts of the world, especially Pakistan and Afghanistan, terrorism, wars and conflicts stop children to go to their schools. We are really tired of these wars. Women and children are suffering in many ways in many parts of the world.

In India, innocent and poor children are victims of child labour. Many schools have been destroyed in Nigeria. People in Afghanistan have been affected by the hurdles of extremism for decades. Young girls have to do domestic child labour and are forced to get married at an early age. Poverty, ignorance, injustice, racism and the deprivation of basic rights are the main problems faced by both men and women.

Today, I am focusing on women's rights and girls' education because they are suffering the most. There was a time when women social activists asked men to stand up for their rights. But this time we will do it by ourselves. I am not telling men to step away from speaking for women's rights, rather I am focusing on women to be independent to fight for themselves.

So, dear sisters and brothers, now it's time to speak up.

So today, we call upon the world leaders to change their strategic policies in favour of peace and prosperity. We call upon the world leaders that all of these deals must protect women and children's rights. A deal that goes against the rights of women is unacceptable.

We call upon all governments to ensure free, compulsory education all over the world for every child.

We call upon all the governments to fight against terrorism and violence. To protect children from brutality and harm.

We call upon the developed nations to support the expansion of education opportunities for girls in the developing world.

We call upon all communities to be tolerant, to reject prejudice based on caste, creed, sect, colour, religion or agenda, to ensure freedom and equality for women so that they can flourish. We cannot all succeed when half of us are held back.

We call upon our sisters around the world to be brave, to embrace the strength within themselves and realize their full potential.

Dear brothers and sisters, we want schools and education for every child's bright future. We will continue our journey to our destination of peace and education. No one can stop us. We will speak up for our rights and we will bring change through our voice.

We believe in the power and the strength of our words. Our words can change the whole world because we are all together, united for the cause of education. And if we want to achieve our goal, then let us empower ourselves with the weapon of knowledge and let us shield ourselves with unity and togetherness.

Dear brothers and sisters, we must not forget that millions of people are suffering from poverty, injustice and ignorance. We must not forget that millions of children are out of their schools. We must not forget that our sisters and brothers are waiting for a bright, peaceful future.

So let us wage a global struggle against illiteracy, poverty and terrorism, let us pick up our books and our pens, they are our most powerful weapons.

One child, one teacher, one book and one pen can change the world. Education is the only solution.

Education first.

KAVITA KRISHNAN

'Freedom Without Fear'

ALL INDIA PROGRESSIVE WOMEN'S ASSOCIATION PROTEST, DELHI

December 2013

In December 2012, a 23-year-old woman named Jyoti Singh was brutally gang raped by six men on a private bus in Delhi. She had been out to see a film with a friend. Less than two weeks later, she died of her injuries.

Indian law doesn't allow a victim's name to be published in the press, so she was referred to in India as 'Nirbhaya' – meaning fearless.

In the following days, huge protests gathered in Delhi and across India. Kavita Krishnan, secretary of the All India Progressive Women's Association and a member of the Communist Party of India (Marxist-Leninist), was one of the most outspoken.

She later described the protests as 'an outburst of accumulated anger against rape culture'.[24] That's exactly what she encapsulated in this searing speech – delivered in Hindi outside the house of India's Chief Minister, Sheila Dikshit – drenched in water after being doused by the water cannons trying to break up the crowds.[25]

Krishnan's rallying cry for women's freedom is not just an outburst of anger. This speech is forensic. She picks apart the different arguments used to blame women – that they are too adventurous, too reckless, or that they need to stay home to stay safe. And she challenged the way arguments about women's 'safety' were being used to limit women's freedom rather than to change the way men – and male-dominated institutions – behave.

Her argument is strong and her demand is clear: 'freedom without fear is what we need'.

The 2012 protests were an explosion of simmering anger. They demonstrated fury at the failure of the authorities to tackle the epidemic of rape and violence against women in India. Women in India are still campaigning for stronger action on violence against women and girls. Last year, the Delhi police reported that five women were raped every day in the capital, and the conviction rate is still alarmingly low.[26]

Sometimes, it can take years of speeches, campaigns and action to deliver change. But Krishnan's words and the 'Nirbhaya' protests of 2013 were a moment of awakening in India and across the world.

And like many of the women featured in the earlier pages of this book, from the abolitionists, to the suffragettes, to the campaigners against extremism, Krishnan's speech wasn't just a moment, it was part of a movement.

Today, we demonstrated outside Sheila Dikshit's house.

Why are we demanding her resignation?

We need people to understand why – it's true that Ms Dikshit made a statement saying the incident occurred on a private bus, not a DTC [Delhi Tourism Corporation] bus, so how could it be her responsibility?

This is what we are here to tell her – if a bus containing iron rods and rapists is plying openly in the city with no rules and regulations, if it can pick up passengers at any time, anywhere – then madam, you are responsible for it, it is no one else's responsibility – it is yours.

If that girl is fighting for her life today, you are responsible for it.

Why was that iron rod in that bus that day – is something that only you can answer, no one else can. You cannot blame anyone else for it.

But there is a more pressing matter than even this – something that we have been talking about, that we are here to talk about today – when that journalist Soumya [Vishwanathan] was murdered, Sheila Dikshit had issued another statement saying, 'If she was out at 3 a.m. in the morning, she was being too adventurous'.

We are here to tell her that women have every right to be adventurous.

We will be adventurous.

We will be reckless.

We will be rash.

Kavita Krishnan

We will do nothing for our safety.

Don't you dare tell us how to dress, when to go out at night, in the day, or how to walk or how many escorts we need!

When Neeraj Kumar was newly appointed as a police commissioner, he held a press conference where he said – look, how can the police do anything about incidents of rape?

The statistic that he presented was that most number of rapes are committed by people known to the woman. This is an authentic statistic – but shouldn't that only make it easier to apprehend the rapist?

Our question for the police is not 'why didn't you prevent this from happening?' But the conviction rate has gone from 46 per cent in 1971 to 26 per cent in 2012 – who is responsible for this?

The fact is that there is a huge gap in the police's investigation, there is an inconsistency – they have no procedure in place for how to deal with a victim of rape. All the women here know that the Delhi Police has only one way of dealing with such a situation – if you were to walk into a police station today and complain that you have been a victim of sexual violence, the first thing they will tell you is not to file a complaint. Strange people will begin to assemble at the station out of nowhere to 'explain' to you – 'beta, don't file a complaint'. […]

I doubt that there is a single woman in Delhi who has gone to the Delhi Police and found otherwise. I don't know which rule book they have adopted this procedure from, but it exists.

Another statement that Neeraj Kumar made at a press conference was that women shouldn't roam around alone, they should have escorts –

and that if you walk around the streets at two in the morning then how can you expect us to come and save you? […]

I believe even if women walk out on the streets alone, even if it is late at night, why should justifications need to be provided for this, like 'she has to work late hours' or 'she was coming home from a BPO job or a media job'? If she simply wants to go out at night, if she wants to go out and buy a cigarette or go for a walk on the road – is this a crime for women? […]

We believe that regardless of whether she is indoors or outside, whether it is day or night, for whatever reason, however she may be dressed – women have a right to freedom. And that freedom without fear is what we need to protect, to guard and respect.

I am saying this because I feel that the word 'safety' with regard to women has been used far too much – all us women know what this 'safety' refers to, we have heard our parents use it, we have heard our communities, our principals, our wardens use it. Women know what 'safety' refers to.

It means – you behave yourself.

You get back into the house.

You don't dress in a particular way.

Do not live by your freedom, and this means that you are safe.

A whole range of patriarchal laws and institutions tell us what to do in the guise of keeping us 'safe'. We reject this entire notion. We don't want it.

The Delhi Police is running an ad campaign about violence against women, you must have seen the large hoardings near ITO, why is there not a single woman in that ad campaign? They have instead a Hindi film actor, Farhan Akhtar, exhorting people 'Be a man, join me in protecting women'.

I want to ask, what about the brother who cuts his sister's head off when she dares to marry into a different community? Is he not playing the role of a male protector too?

This machismo is not any solution to the problem of violence against women; it is, in fact, the root of the problem. This is what we need to understand.

It's clear that in this country, if you leave out the women's movement, the government, the police, the political parties, the judiciary; when they speak of women's 'safety' they are speaking from within a specific patriarchal understanding of the term.

No one is talking about protecting her freedom to live without fear.

LUPITA NYONG'O

'Being Beautiful Inside'

ESSENCE MAGAZINE'S BLACK WOMEN IN HOLLYWOOD, LOS ANGELES

February 2014

Lupita Nyong'o won an Oscar for her first role in a feature film after leaving drama school. It was a nuanced and deeply moving portrayal of Patsey, a slave from the mid-nineteenth century who was repeatedly raped and tortured, in the most powerful film about slavery for a generation, *12 Years A Slave*. In her Oscar acceptance speech, she said:

> It doesn't escape me for one moment that so much joy in my life is thanks to so much pain in someone else's. And so I want to salute the spirit of Patsey for her guidance.[27]

Nyong'o draws on Patsey's story as well as her own in this speech to *Essence* magazine's Black Women in Hollywood event in 2014, as she describes being taunted as a child for her 'night-shaded skin'.

The speech starts with a heartbreaking letter from a young black girl who had considered using skin whitening products before she saw Nyong'o on the screen, and Nyong'o relates to that feeling of self-loathing – of having felt 'un-beautiful' as a child due to the colour of her skin. It was only when she saw black supermodel Alek Wek, and the women who starred in the film adaptation of Alice Walker's groundbreaking novel, *The Colour Purple*, that she saw a reflection of herself that made her feel proud.

Nyong'o used this speech to tell young girls who might be listening that they are beautiful and worthy, the very words she needed to hear as a child who felt ugly in her skin. But her wider message is that beauty is not something that can be acquired but something that you just have to be. What fundamentally sustains us, Nyong'o beautifully explains, 'is compassion for yourself' – it is that kind of beauty which 'enchants the soul'.

It is an effective speech in so many ways; Nyong'o moves deftly from the story of the young girl who wrote to her, to her own story, to her wider message and then back to Patsey's story at the end, making each stage of the speech compelling by doing so. She has a simple truth at the core of her speech – that what matters is beauty on the inside. But woven all around it are reflections on racism and on the oppressive expectations on girls to meet particular standards of physical 'beauty', as well as a direct challenge to the industry in which she works and a comment on the damaging lack of diversity in the fashion and entertainment industries.

In October 2017, Nyong'o joined other actresses who were

speaking out as part of the #MeToo movement, chronicling the sexual harassment she had experienced from Harvey Weinstein, how he had threatened her career when she refused his advances. She wrote:

> Now that we are speaking, let us never shut up about this kind of thing. I speak up to make certain that this is not the kind of misconduct that deserves a second chance. I speak up to contribute to the end of the conspiracy of silence.[28]

In those words, and in this speech from 2014, you get that sense that Nyong'o understands the power she holds as a celebrity and role model, and is determined to shape the world for the better. And at the same time, she stresses how much she owes to others – showing humility and grace in her speeches as she pays tribute to those whose struggles have made it possible for her to speak out now.

But perhaps what makes Nyong'o's speech most effective of all is that she makes it feel personal not just for herself but for her audience. It's clear who she most wants to hear her words, and she never loses sight of them – in this case the young black girls to whom she speaks directly at the end of the speech – sharing her hope that they will feel the validation of their external beauty, but more importantly, that they will focus on being beautiful on the inside.

I received a letter from a girl, and I'd like to share just a small part of it with you.

'Dear Lupita,' it reads, 'I think you're really lucky to be this black but yet this successful in Hollywood overnight. I was just about to buy Dencia's Whitenicious cream to lighten my skin, when you appeared on the world map and saved me.'

My heart bled a little when I read those words. I could never have guessed that my first job out of school would be so powerful, in and of itself, and that it would propel me to be such an image of hope in the same way that the women of *The Colour Purple* were to me.

I remember a time when I too felt un-beautiful. I put on the TV and only saw pale skin. I got teased and taunted about my night-shaded skin. And my one prayer to God, the miracle worker, was that I would wake up lighter skinned. The morning would come and I would be so excited about seeing my new skin, that I would refuse to look down at myself until I was in front of a mirror because I wanted to see my fair face first.

And every day I experienced the same disappointment of being just as dark as I had been the day before.

I tried to negotiate with God. I told him I would stop stealing sugar cubes at night if he gave me what I wanted. I would listen to my mother's every word, and never lose my school sweater again – if he just made me a little lighter. But, I guess God was unimpressed with my bargaining chips because he never listened. And when I was a teenager, my self-hate grew worse, as you can imagine happens with adolescents.

My mother reminded me often that she thought I was beautiful. But that was no consolation, she's my mother. Of course, she's supposed to think I'm beautiful. And then, Alek Wek came on the international scene as a celebrated model. She was dark as night. She was on all the runways and in every magazine and everyone was talking about how beautiful she was, even Oprah called her beautiful and that made it a fact.

I couldn't believe that people were embracing a woman who looked so much like me as beautiful. My complexion had always been an obstacle to overcome, and all of a sudden Oprah was telling me it wasn't. It was perplexing and I wanted to reject it because I had begun to enjoy the seduction of inadequacy. But, a flower couldn't help but bloom inside me.

When I saw Alek, I inadvertently saw a reflection of myself that I could not deny. Now, I had a spring in my step because I felt more seen. More appreciated by the far-away gatekeepers of beauty.

But around me, the preference for light skin prevailed. To the beholders that I thought mattered, I was still unbeautiful. And my mother, again, would say to me, you can't eat beauty. It doesn't feed you. And these words played and bothered me. I didn't really understand them until finally I realized that beauty was not a thing that I could acquire or consume, it was something that I just had to be.

And what my mother meant when she said you can't eat beauty was that you can't rely on how you look to sustain you. What actually sustains us, what is fundamentally beautiful, is compassion for yourself, and for those around you. That kind of beauty inflames the heart and enchants the soul. It is what got Patsey in so much trouble with her master. But it is also what has kept her story alive to this day. We remember the beauty of her spirit, even after the beauty of her body has faded away.

And so, I hope that my presence on your screens and in magazines may lead you, young girl, on a similar journey. That you will feel the validation of your external beauty, but also get to the deeper business of being beautiful inside.

There is no shade in that beauty.

"

HARRIET HARMAN

'Parliament Must Lead by Example'

LONDON

July 2014

I first met Harriet Harman in Blackpool at the 1992 Labour Party Conference. It was a job interview and I was supposed to meet her outside the Winter Garden, but I didn't know which entrance. So when I saw her rush round the corner towards a different door I chased after her, shouting, promptly fell over, laddered my tights and grazed my knee.

Harriet was motherly. She took me straight to Marks & Spencer to buy new tights then conducted the interview over a cup of tea in a corner of the conference centre. Within twenty minutes – she had somewhere else she had to be – she had concluded: 'Yes, I think you'd better start.' It never felt like I had a choice.

That first encounter with Harriet captured her personality – busy, supportive, unconventional, hugely practical, never taking no for an answer. The encouragement and help she has given me over the twenty-five years I've known her have been immense – from personal support when I got ill in my twenties and had to take a year off work, to helping me battle with the obstacles of ministerial maternity leave in my thirties. Many other women in politics have similar stories to tell.

When she was elected in a by-election in 1982, not only was she one of only ten Labour women in Parliament, she was also heavily pregnant. And not only did she blaze a personal trail that made it much easier for other women to follow, she was also uncompromising in her determination to keep raising the practical concerns of women across the country.

She challenged Margaret Thatcher in Parliament on childcare. She was one of the leading advocates of the All Women Shortlists adopted by the Labour Party that brought a massive increase in the number of women MPs. In government she led action on domestic violence, childcare, maternity leave and pay, and drew up the 2010 Equality Act. And as Deputy Leader of the Labour Party and now Mother of the House of Commons (longest-serving woman MP), she has continually used her seniority to encourage other women to get on or campaign for change. Her determination never to accept the status quo, and always to be restless in the fight for equality, mean that she has ruffled feathers and made enemies. But that hasn't stopped her.

This speech, given as a lecture in the Speaker's reception rooms in Parliament, summed up her focused and passionate approach to equality and discrimination that has underpinned so much of her work. She was scathing about the idea that you can pit equality against merit, or that more women means losing better men. As she pointed out:

> How could it have been the result of merit or quality that when I arrived in 1982 Parliament was 97 per cent men and only 3 per cent women?

She argued strongly for more black and Asian MPs, more working-class MPs, more disabled MPs – 'when people see Parliament on TV it's important that they see people like themselves' – but she also argued strongly against creating hierarchies that pit different kinds of inequality against each other, and called for everyone to make common cause.

I chose this particular one out of Harriet's many speeches because it's the perfect overview of the pioneering work she's done. But it misses one important line that I heard her say many times in speeches across the country, which should be a reassurance to all the women who speak out but then face resistance, and which best sums Harriet up:

> If you are not having arguments you are probably not making a difference.[29]

My starting point is the basic principle. The principle of equality – that no one should be excluded from, or discriminated against in, representing a constituency, becoming an MP, because they're a woman, because they're not white, because they are gay, disabled or from a working-class background. Parliament must represent all of the people so it must champion equality. It cannot do that if, by its composition, it's an emblem of inequality.

Parliament must include the best people – drawn from the widest pool of talent and commitment. It is not doing that if it's exclusive and discriminatory. So it's paradoxical that our argument for equality in the composition of Parliament meets with resistance on the basis that it would water down the 'quality' of MPs. MPs are chosen on merit – we were told – and what we were arguing for was a threat to that.

But how could it have been the result of merit or quality that, when I arrived in 1982, Parliament was 97 per cent men and only 3 per cent women. And this overwhelmingly male Parliament was 100 per cent white. … The argument that pits merit against equality is ludicrous, and also offensive. It tells women, black people, people with disabilities and from working-class backgrounds, 'we'd like to have you here but we can't afford to water down the quality'.

What matters is not just the quality of the individuals but also the composition of the institution as a whole. And even if the individuals are high quality, if they are totally homogenous then the institution as a whole lacks merit.

When people see Parliament on TV it's important that they see and hear people like themselves. How could women believe that an overwhelmingly male Parliament understood their lives? How shameful that for so many years people from the Asian and Afro-Caribbean communities had played their part so assiduously in our democracy by voting in general elections and yet not one single MP was non-white.

When Bernie Grant – who along with Diane Abbott was one of two Afro-Caribbean MPs to come into Parliament in 1987 – appeared at the Queen's Speech dressed in full African dress there were sneers. But to see him there – resplendent in flowing African robes on the Green benches of the House of Commons – sent a huge positive message to the Afro-Caribbean community, not least in my constituency [of Camberwell and Peckham] – that the House of Commons was now hearing from them. […]

The election of David Blunkett not only brought a great politician to Parliament, it sent a powerful message that Parliament would hear from people with disabilities and recognize their abilities. Every time Anne Begg spoke from her wheelchair in the Commons it was not only about the importance of what she said but also about the inclusion of wheelchair users more generally. […]

To lead the fight against inequality, Parliament must lead by example. It cannot hope to lead change to tackle inequality in the country, if it itself embodies discrimination. […]

Diversity means class background too. The Labour Party was founded to speak up for working-class communities. But the founding PLP [Parliamentary Labour Party] – being disproportionately university graduates – was initially very different from the trade union members in whose interests the party was established. But through the Labour Party, the trade union movement did, for many years, bring to Parliament men from working-class backgrounds. […]

It is a challenge to our party to select candidates from all different backgrounds. And with more than 50 per cent of the trade union members being women, that must mean working-class women as well. […]

The political agenda is shaped by who's in Parliament. Despite pioneers like Jo Richardson, issues like childcare and domestic violence scarcely made a dent on the political agenda before the women MPs arrived in 1997. It needed Dawn Primarolo to move an amendment to the 2000 Finance Bill to exempt sanitary towels from VAT. No man in Parliament at that time could even bring himself to mention periods. […]

Though my election to Parliament was because of the demand of the women's movement to redress the lack of women in Parliament, as soon as I arrived I was under pressure to be just like the men. As a fish out of water, one of only ten Labour women in a Parliament of over 600 MPs, I received well-meaning advice on how I could redress my deficiencies.

I should keep my head down for a few years, and learn the ropes. I should avoid the terrible humiliation that would befall me if I made a mistake. I must avoid drawing attention to myself. It would only annoy everyone. I should not 'bang on' about women or I'd be pigeonholed and stereotyped, so I should focus on mainstream issues. And I should hang out in the bar to show I was 'clubbable'.

But having supported me to get into Parliament, the women's movement wanted me to blaze a trail – and would have been dismayed if I'd kept my head down. … It was impossible to be inconspicuous when I arrived hugely pregnant. And I couldn't hang out in the bar when I was feeling sick from pregnancy or rushing home to put the babies to bed.

Because I didn't conform, the punishment for being different was often nasty. When I came back after having my first baby I was reported to the sergeant-at-arms for breaking the rules by taking my baby through the division lobby under my jacket. Of course I'd done no such thing – I was still fat from being pregnant. Once I told the whips I'd have to miss a vote because I was ill – with mastitis. And they put it in the papers.

My campaign for more women MPs was deeply resented by the men MPs who accused me of attacking them by implying they were incapable of representing their women constituents. […]

Our campaigns for more women MPs succeeded. Only through the mechanism of All Women Shortlists. … We had tried bringing about change by winning the argument – making the case to select more women. We tried a woman on every shortlist for selection. We tried fifty–fifty shortlists. But it was only by the radical measure of excluding men altogether from 50 per cent of the seats we hoped to win, that we got women elected.

The effect of those All Women Shortlists was transformational – more than 100 Labour women swept into Parliament in 1997. That changed not just the face of Parliament but the agenda of politics.

We introduced the National Childcare Strategy, new laws on domestic violence, the Equality Act, doubled maternity pay and leave, brought in the right to request flexible working – issues of huge importance to women in this country. […]

But even with a critical mass of Labour women MPs – they still face challenges. Not least around the issue of children. A woman MP is defined by her marital status and reproductive record in a way that would be unthinkable for a man. … Bake cookies and you are a real woman – but can't be a leader. Fail to bake cookies and you can be a leader, but you're not a real woman. […]

A woman MP with children is either a devoted mother and a deficient MP, or a dynamic and ambitious MP and therefore a deficient mother.

An MP father who attends his child's school open evening is admired as heroic. But a woman MP best not mention it because she'll be identified as insufficiently committed to her work. And this is because the underlying reality and the cultural expectation is that in most families, it's still the mother who takes the daily responsibility for young children – and for older relatives. […]

And the truth is that even getting to the top of the political structures is no guarantee of equality. Imagine my surprise when, having won a hard-fought election to succeed John Prescott as deputy leader of the Labour Party, I discovered that I was not to succeed him as deputy prime minister!

If one of the men had won the deputy leadership would that have happened? Would they have put up with it? I doubt it. […]

Parliament needs to be more ethnically diverse, more representative of people with disabilities and include more people from working-class backgrounds. In the quest for progress, some argue that race discrimination is much more vicious and intractable than discrimination against women. That All Women Shortlists have discriminated against black men. Some argue that it is your class background which matters above all. That middle-class women squeeze out working-class men.

We have to guard against the danger of pitting one sort of inequality against another. Fighting amongst ourselves to establish a hierarchy of inequalities is self-defeating. The issues are different, but they all matter.

We need to make common cause, not succumb to divide and rule.

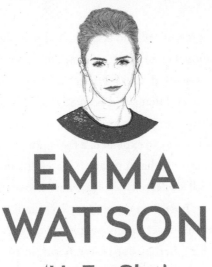

EMMA WATSON

'HeForShe'

UNITED NATIONS, NEW YORK
September 2014

Emma Watson grew up playing *Harry Potter* heroine Hermione Granger. When Ban Ki-moon introduced her to the United Nations in 2014, he said: 'You've been waving a magic wand in your movies… I hope you use your magic wand to end violence against women.' In the absence of a wand, Watson used her words.

The speech marked the launch of the UN's #HeForShe campaign, which called on men to be allies in the feminist cause. The speech has been watched over 5 million times on YouTube, and while Watson's fame may have attracted many of those initial viewers, especially younger ones, the speech itself gained notoriety because of its clear message:

Gender equality is your issue too.

Her delivery is measured and serious, and her speech makes no assumptions about her audience's views. She isn't aiming her words at the already converted, she is setting out to persuade.

Watson later said that she'd been advised not to use the word 'feminist' at all in the speech, but realizing that was precisely the problem, she goes out of her way to explain in a thoughtful way why she calls herself a feminist and what it means.[30] Carefully, she lists personal experiences which led her to challenge gender stereotypes: at age eight being described as bossy, at fourteen being sexualized by the press.

And it had an impact. Many people felt they'd grown up with Watson, watching her, as our children did, in the Harry Potter films. So then young women from across the world saw the speech and felt empowered to use the word feminist, reclaiming it as a positive and powerful one. Even Malala, who had publicly been campaigning for girls' education for several years, later told Watson that she'd found the word 'feminist' a tricky one before watching Watson's speech: 'I hesitated in saying am I feminist or not? Then after hearing your speech I decided … there's nothing wrong by calling yourself a feminist.'[31]

Young actors or artists who make the leap from the dramatic to the political stage often face a backlash. Their fame may make it harder for their opponents to silence them, but the decision to speak out is still a daunting one, and their status doesn't protect them from the vitriol that inevitably follows. Watson said that the speech led to 'a level of critique I had never experienced in my life and the beginning of a series of threats'.[32]

But as she says in this speech, she had asked herself, like many of the women in this compilation would have done before and since:

If not me, who? If not now, when?

Today we are launching a campaign called 'HeForShe'.

I am reaching out to you because I need your help. We want to end gender inequality – and to do that we need everyone to be involved.

This is the first campaign of its kind at the UN: we want to try and galvanize as many men and boys as possible to be advocates for gender equality. And we don't just want to talk about it, but make sure it is tangible.

I was appointed as Goodwill Ambassador for UN Women six months ago and the more I have spoken about feminism the more I have realized that fighting for women's rights has too often become synonymous with man-hating. If there is one thing I know for certain, it is that this has to stop.

For the record, feminism by definition is: 'The belief that men and women should have equal rights and opportunities. It is the theory of the political, economic and social equality of the sexes.'

I started questioning gender-based assumptions when at eight I was confused at being called 'bossy', because I wanted to direct the plays we would put on for our parents – but the boys were not.

When at fourteen I started being sexualized by certain elements of the press.

When at fifteen my girlfriends started dropping out of their sports teams because they didn't want to appear 'muscly'.

When at eighteen my male friends were unable to express their feelings.

I decided I was a feminist and this seemed uncomplicated to me. But my recent research has shown me that feminism has become an unpopular word. Apparently I am among the ranks of women whose expressions are seen as too strong, too aggressive, isolating, anti-men and unattractive.

Why is the word such an uncomfortable one?

I am from Britain and think it is right that as a woman I am paid the same as my male counterparts. I think it is right that I should be able to make decisions about my own body. I think it is right that women be involved on my behalf in the policies and decision-making of my country. I think it is right that socially I am afforded the same respect as men. But sadly I can say that there is no one country in the world where all women can expect to receive these rights.

No country in the world can yet say they have achieved gender equality.

These rights I consider to be human rights, but I am one of the lucky ones. My life is a sheer privilege because my parents didn't love me less because I was born a daughter. My school did not limit me because I was a girl. My mentors didn't assume I would go less far because I might give birth to a child one day. These influencers were the gender equality ambassadors that made me who I am today. They may not know it, but they are the inadvertent feminists who are changing the world today. And we need more of those.

And if you still hate the word – it is not the word that is important but the idea and the ambition behind it. Because not all women have been afforded the same rights that I have. In fact, statistically, very few have been.

In 1995, Hillary Clinton made a famous speech in Beijing about women's rights. Sadly many of the things she wanted to change are still a reality today.

But what stood out for me the most was that only 30 per cent of her audience were male. How can we effect change in the world when only half of it is invited or feels welcome to participate in the conversation?

Men – I would like to take this opportunity to extend your formal invitation. Gender equality is your issue too.

Because to date, I've seen my father's role as a parent being valued less by society, despite my needing his presence as a child as much as my mother's. I've seen young men suffering from mental illness unable to ask for help for fear it would make them look less 'macho' – in fact in the UK suicide is the biggest killer of men between twenty and forty-nine years of age; eclipsing road accidents, cancer and coronary heart disease. I've seen men made fragile and insecure by a distorted sense of what constitutes male success. Men don't have the benefits of equality either.

We don't often talk about men being imprisoned by gender stereotypes but I can see that they are and that when they are free, things will change for women as a natural consequence. If men don't have to be aggressive in order to be accepted, women won't feel compelled to be submissive. If men don't have to control, women won't have to be controlled.

Both men and women should feel free to be sensitive. Both men and women should feel free to be strong… It is time that we all perceive gender on a spectrum, not as two opposing sets of ideals.

If we stop defining each other by what we are not and start defining ourselves by what we are – we can all be freer and this is what HeForShe is about. It's about freedom.

I want men to take up this mantle. So their daughters, sisters and mothers can be free from prejudice but also so that their sons have permission to be vulnerable and human too – reclaim those parts of themselves they abandoned and in doing so be a more true and complete version of themselves.

You might be thinking, who is this *Harry Potter* girl? And what is she doing up on stage at the UN. It's a good question and trust me, I have been asking myself the same thing. I don't know if I am qualified to be here. All I know is that I care about this problem. And I want to make it better.

And having seen what I've seen – and given the chance – I feel it is my duty to say something. English statesman Edmund Burke said: 'All that is needed for the forces of evil to triumph is for enough good men and women to do nothing.'

In my nervousness for this speech and in my moments of doubt I've told myself firmly – if not me, who; if not now, when. If you have similar doubts when opportunities are presented to you, I hope those words might be helpful.

Because the reality is that if we do nothing it will take seventy-five years, or for me to be nearly a hundred, before women can expect to be paid the same as men for the same work. 15.5 million girls will be married in the next sixteen years as children. And at current rates it won't be until 2086 before all rural African girls will be able to receive a secondary education.

If you believe in equality, you might be one of those inadvertent feminists I spoke of earlier.

And for this I applaud you.

We are struggling for a uniting word but the good news is we have a uniting movement. It is called HeForShe. I am inviting you to step forward, to be seen to speak up, to be the 'he' for 'she'. And to ask yourself: if not me, who? If not now, when?

"

JO COX
'More in Common'

HOUSE OF COMMONS
June 2015

Jo Cox loved life. She grabbed it, hugged it, bounced it around, and made it joyous for those who knew her. Jo was a friend and for just twelve months before she died she was a colleague – a fellow West Yorkshire Labour MP elected for her home town of Batley. This introduction is hard to write.

Passionate, creative, forceful, funny, Jo did nothing by halves. She threw herself into knotty problems, made friends, pulled people together and bravely took on tough causes. In a short time in Parliament she had a big impact, drawing on her experience as an international aid worker to press the government for humanitarian support for Syria and developing cross-party work to tackle loneliness.

It's her laughter I remember most – that and her fierce love for her family and two young children. Jo loved any chance to hold a party, to bring people together or make new friends.

Jo's maiden speech was a classic of its kind – a tribute to her predecessor, a celebration of her constituency, a bit of the historical, a bit of the personal, a bit of the political: Jo takes us on a tour from Fox's biscuits to fish and chips to curries.

However, framing the speech is one important thought that reflects Jo's core philosophy, and which was to prove painfully prescient. As she described the diverse communities that make up the constituency of Batley and Spen, she said, 'we are far more united and have far more in common than that which divides us'.

On 16 June 2016, at the height of the Brexit referendum campaign, Jo was killed on her way to her constituency surgery by a far-right extremist.

We all lost her far too soon. That night many of us gathered at St Peter's Church in Birstall – friends, neighbours, constituents, to grieve together. And Jo was right. People came from diverse communities to share common love for Jo and her family, our horror and distress at what had happened and our deep sadness at what we had lost.

In the years since Jo died, her friends and family have set up a remarkable foundation in her name to promote her causes and values including a commission on loneliness, backed by the government, to help those in need of company or friends, and support for the White Helmets saving lives in Syria.

But perhaps most powerfully in memory of Jo, they have set up the Great Get Together – a weekend when communities across the country come together, to fight against the hatred that killed Jo and remember what we have in common instead.

Thank you, Mr Speaker; it is a great privilege to be called to make my maiden speech in this most important of debates, and I congratulate many others who have made outstanding maiden speeches today.

I am sure that many right hon. and hon. Members will claim that their constituencies consist of two halves or numerous parochial parts; I am another in that respect, and Batley and Spen is very much that kind of constituency. It is a joy to represent such a diverse community.

Batley and Spen is a gathering of typically independent, no-nonsense and proud Yorkshire towns and villages. Our communities have been deeply enhanced by immigration, be it of Irish Catholics across the constituency or of Muslims from Gujarat in India or from Pakistan, principally from Kashmir.

While we celebrate our diversity, what surprises me time and time again as I travel around the constituency is that we are far more united and have far more in common than that which divides us.

My constituency is also home to Fox's Biscuits and Lion Confectionery, so I am sure you will not think it an indulgence, Mr Speaker, if I describe Batley and Spen as a constituency with an industrial heart wrapped in a very rich and pleasant Yorkshire landscape – geographical, historical and cultural.

The spirit of nonconformity is as prevalent now in my part of West Yorkshire as it was in the time of my two immediate predecessors, Mike Wood and Elizabeth Peacock. They were both known for offering their own brand of independent, nonconformist service, albeit in very different ways. I intend to maintain that established tradition in my own unique style.

Of course, Batley is a town that has sent Labour MPs to this place for the best part of a hundred years. One of them, Dr Broughton, is of course famously credited with bringing down a government, so I respectfully put the right hon. Members on the frontbench opposite on notice.

The Spen Valley has a far more chequered political history, alternately sending Labour and Conservative MPs here to Westminster for much of the twentieth century. Nothing made me prouder on 8 May than to be sent to this place with an increased Labour majority, proving again that in my neck of the woods nonconformity is what we do best.

As I have already alluded to, we make things in Batley and Spen; we do so now, just as we did historically. Batley and Spen has a high proportion of people working in manufacturing, and we can boast the full range of industries, including high-skilled, precision engineering. We manufacture all sorts, from beds to biscuits, and from carpets to lathes. We also have some of the best fish and chips in the country, and some of the best curries in the world.

However, what many of our businesses are lacking is confidence: confidence to expand; confidence to borrow; confidence to grow; and the confidence to fuel a real economic recovery that benefits everybody, offering decent jobs, paying decent wages and bridging the skills gap.

Key to changing that situation is a fundamental shift in attitude towards regional economic regeneration. It is time to give city and county regions the powers and resources they need to promote growth, and

I will happily work with all of those who are genuinely committed to building an economic powerhouse in the north.

This agenda has to have at its centre a commitment to connect towns and villages in constituencies like mine to thriving city hubs, and to deliver a financial offer in the forthcoming July Budget that gives this worthy goal a real chance of success.

Yorkshire folk are not fools: talk about devolving power to cities and regions, while simultaneously stripping them of the resources to deliver and subjecting northern councils such as Kirklees to the harshest of cuts, is not compatible with a worthy commitment to building a northern powerhouse to drive growth and prosperity.

Businesses in my constituency want help to address the skills mismatch at local level which leaves employers with staff shortages and young people without jobs. They want access to reliable sources of finance, including a network of local banks.

They want to connect to a regional infrastructure that works for them, not rail price hikes of more than 126 per cent and endless delays to key transport projects such as the electrification of the line from Manchester to Leeds.

Many businesses in Yorkshire want the security and stability of Britain's continued membership of the European Union, a cause I look forward to championing passionately in this place and elsewhere.

The key question is: will the government's actions match their northern powerhouse rhetoric? HS2 is not the only acid test. There are two bigger challenges. First, will the government really devolve all the powers and decisions that could and should be taken locally and regionally? My test will be this: if there is a compelling reason for this to be a national decision then so be it; if not, it should be devolved.

Secondly, will the government really take the whole range of their decisions - on transport, research and development, planning, education and skills - in the interests of rebalancing the economy and growing the north?

I am Batley and Spen born and bred, and I could not be prouder of that.

I am proud that I was made in Yorkshire and I am proud of the things we make in Yorkshire. Britain should be proud of that, too.

I look forward to representing the great people of Batley and Spen here over the next five years.

99

YVETTE
COOPER

'Britain Has to Play Our Part'

LONDON

September 2015

I spent the summer of 2015 making speeches. But this one was different.

We were in the middle of the Labour leadership election. As one of four candidates standing, I had been travelling the country in an endless cycle of hustings, media interviews, rallies and community events that involved giving speeches on inequality, childcare, public services and the future of our party. Barely did any of us pause for breath. Most of our hustings and speeches involved attacks on the Conservative government, ideas about the future of the Labour Party, or policy disagreements with each other.

Then on 27 August a deeply disturbing story hit the news. Austrian police had opened a lorry that had sat at the side of a motorway for several days. They found seventy-one people from Syria, Iraq and Afghanistan – including a toddler and a seven-year-old girl – suffocated inside. They had been locked inside the van by people traffickers who had exploited their desperation to flee persecution and conflict and to find a better life.

Throughout that year, the Syrian refugee crisis had been escalating – 8 million people had already been forced to leave their homes. Lebanon had just closed its border having already taken in over a million refugees. Camps in Turkey and Jordan were becoming ever more crowded. Traffickers and smuggler gangs were making money from misery. Things were becoming ever more unstable and lives were at risk. People were taking to small boats – flimsy black dinghies – to cross the Mediterranean. But British and European governments seemed to have no idea how to respond. It was an issue I'd done a lot of work on the previous year, but that summer my focus had been elsewhere until that story of the Austrian lorry.

I found it hard to stop thinking about families being packed into sealed containers struggling to breathe. And about the cars of commuters, holiday makers, traders, all whizzing by, unaware as people died. I knew I had to say something. I knew we needed pressure on the British government and on European governments to act.

By this time the leadership campaign was drawing to a close. Jeremy Corbyn was already well ahead, but all of us in the campaign still had a profile and a platform, and we had an opportunity to be heard. So I cancelled my previous campaign plans and started writing this speech instead. It had to be different from the normal speeches we had all been making. Instead of attacking the government or challenging the other candidates, I knew we had to try to build some consensus on the action needed so that Britain could play its part. I didn't expect it to be easy. Often the debate muddled up immigration and asylum. And I didn't want legitimate disagreements over different immigration rules for employment or students to overshadow help for those fleeing persecution.

But unlike other speeches I've written, this one felt like it wrote itself. I knew what I wanted to say and who I wanted to persuade. I wanted to appeal to everyone across the parties to come forward to help – to make this a common endeavour. I knew it wouldn't happen if it was politicized; on this we needed consensus. I included a long list of policies I thought were needed from countries across the world working together – from action against trafficking gangs to aiding refugee camps in the Middle East. I wanted to show it was sensible and manageable, that our country had done it before. And most of all, I wanted to appeal to the best of us, to the best of being British.

I also knew that to wake people up I couldn't duck the most difficult issue and I had to put a number on the refugees Britain would resettle. So I asked councils to come forward with suggestions and proposed 10,000 over a year – the number of refugees we could resettle if every city or county helped ten families. I expected a backlash, and of course there was one online. But mostly I was struck by the level of support from across the country and across the political spectrum.

The following day, 3 August 2015, a shocking photo appeared. A child's body had been swept up on a Turkish beach. Aylan Kurdi, just four years old, had drowned with his mother when the dinghy they were on sank. As we all stared at the picture of a little boy in shorts and sneakers, lying lifeless on a beach, the clamour for action suddenly rose.

Initially the government said it wasn't possible for Britain to resettle more refugees, but public and political pressure grew and as the Scottish and Welsh governments and local councils from all political parties offered to help, so too did charities and faith groups. The unthinkable suddenly became possible. Four days later Prime Minister David Cameron announced that Britain would offer places for 20,000 Syrian refugees over the next few years. Since then I've met many Syrian families across the country who are rebuilding their lives here in Britain; families being welcomed by local communities, getting their kids back into schools, learning English, starting work. Britain's resettlement scheme is still limited compared to many other countries, but for those desperate families, it has given them back a future.

Over the past twenty years I have made many speeches on major issues – Labour Party Conference speeches to big crowds on housing or policing, speeches at the Fabian Society on the future of Labour or the challenges facing our towns, ministerial speeches announcing legislation to end child poverty or roll out Sure Start, and parliamentary debates on equal marriage, immigration or Brexit. Of all those speeches I chose this one, not because it was my best written, or even compared to ministerial speeches the one that affected most lives. I chose it because it was a turning point. Its significance lay in its timing and not in my oratory. It was the tragic photo of Aylan Kurdi the next day that galvanized everyone. But I hope this speech helped shape the national response and helped the government do the right thing – I hope it helped reinforce the power of a picture with the power of words.

By the side of an Austrian road, a lorry. A logo on the side. Designed to transport 'original Slovenian products' – ham and chicken. In a sealed fridge. Inside, seventy-one bodies.

Seventy-one people. It looks like they came from Syria. Families. Children. A little girl just two years old. They must have travelled through Turkey or Greece, through the Balkans, Hungary; many days' journey by road.

Maybe they came from Homs where just a few weeks ago 200 innocent men, women and children were kidnapped by ISIL. Maybe they came from camps where thousands are living in desert tents without running water, proper schooling or medical care.

Who knows how much they paid the traffickers who put them in the lorry, sealed the fridge door and drove off while they suffocated to death. A truly terrible story. And all the more terrible because it isn't unique.

Just two days later three children were found close to death from dehydration in the back of a crowded minivan. Fifty-two people were found dead in the hull of a boat; beaten by the smugglers into an airless hold; required to pay money to come up to breathe. Those that couldn't, suffocated to death. A hundred people were found drowned, locked in the hold of a capsized boat.

Even on our own doorstep, nine people have died in the last three months trying to cross from Calais to Dover – trapped on the wheel arches of lorries, crushed jumping onto fast-moving trains or electrocuted on power lines. Terrible stories of tragedy, torture, desperation.

But the tragic stories are not just of those who have died. There are millions more who have lost their homes and are now desperately seeking sanctuary or stability to rebuild their lives. The exhausted mother desperately holding her baby's head above the waves. The children who have had no schooling for months. The former teachers, office workers, shop owners, business people – now refugees, sleeping in bus stations, paying gangs to ferry them by night.

This has become a humanitarian crisis on a scale we have not seen on our continent since the Second World War. Yet we seem paralysed to respond. Stuck in the troubled politics of immigration when this is about asylum instead. Stuck treating immigration and asylum as the same thing when they are completely different and we should keep them so. Stuck in disputes over student visas, illegal working or European agency workers when none of that has anything to do with refugees. Stuck talking only about 'migrants' when we should mean fathers, sons, sisters, brothers, daughters, mothers. Stuck in political cowardice that assumes British voters' unease about immigration means they will not forgive anyone who calls for sanctuary – even though our nation has given shelter to the persecuted for centuries …

And it's not just us. All Europe is struggling to respond. We can't carry on like this. It's immoral, it's cowardly and it's not the British way. Hundreds of thousands of refugees are fleeing from a new totalitarianism and Europe has to help – just as we did in generations past. We should be strong enough and resilient enough to rise to the challenge, not turn our backs. But we can only do that together.

So I'm not going to make the normal political speech either as Shadow Home Secretary or as Labour leadership candidate – attacking the government and setting out an alternative Labour response. Because I don't want to attack others over this, I want to persuade everyone.

I don't want this to be a party-political row because I want our British government to show leadership now – and I want the Labour Party, all parties, cities, towns and communities across the country to support them when they do. ... We can make it possible for our government to do what is right. But to do so we have to speak out. [...]

According to the UN, a third of a million people have tried to cross the Mediterranean in the last eight months. ... At least 2,600 have died – drowned or suffocated on the voyage. ... The UN estimate that more than half of those crossing the Mediterranean are from Syria. ... What many are fleeing is a new totalitarianism of our time; from ISIL and Islamist extremists – a doctrine that promotes terrifying violence in the name of ideology ... We have a moral responsibility to do our bit to help those who flee to survive.

We have a responsibility too to stop the abuse of human rights on our continent – to stop the criminal gangs, the modern slave traders operating in Europe, who are driving much of the desperate travel, the terrible conditions and the abuse and deaths. ... It is a heartless violation of the basic human rights we fought past wars to defend. And we have a responsibility to make sure there is safety, security and order, both at our borders and in the asylum system or public confidence won't be maintained. We cannot carry on like this. We cannot allow the politics of fear and blame to paralyse us and let this humanitarian crisis go on. It's time to act. [...]

First, we need smarter coordination and deployment of EU aid to help prevent the scale of travel and trafficking in the first place – supporting people in the region so that in the end they can return home. [...]

Second, we need stronger and more effective measures against the vile people-trafficking trade – to rescue those at risk and stop the criminal gangs. [...] More safety and security checks are needed. [...]

Third, we need major investment in asylum and immigration assessment – including centres established overseas and at the European border. […]

Fourth, and perhaps toughest of all, we need all European countries to sign up to take in those agreed to be in need of refuge or asylum. … We need each country to come forward urgently with their own assessment of how much support they can provide – and Britain needs to play our part. […]

As a country we have a long and proud history of offering to those in need. In the 1680s, 50,000 Huguenots clambered aboard boats in La Rochelle [bound for England] to escape persecution by the French state. Two hundred years later, over 140,000 refugees made their way to Britain escaping the oppression of the Russian Czar. In the thirties, despite recession and hardship, we took in over 80,000 Jewish and European refugees. In the nineties, we took in refugees from Bosnia.

This year we marked the death of Sir Nicholas Winton – the man who helped arrange the Kindertransport … to offer sanctuary to Jewish children from Germany and Nazi-occupied territory. … Over nine months, 10,000 children came to the UK from across Germany, Austria, Czechoslovakia and Poland. Ten thousand.

What are we doing now?

Our country has refused to take any refugees from the Mediterranean, has refused to take more than a couple of hundred vulnerable Syrian refugees directly from the camps as part of the UN programme. Just 240 have come. And our country has even returned Syrian refugees to other European countries who are already taking far more refugees, simply because they passed through those countries first. … How can we be proud of our history of helping those who fled conflict if our generation turns its back?

So it is time to ask cities, towns, communities how much they each can do to help. If every city took ten refugee families, if every London borough took ten families, if every county council took ten families, if Scotland, Wales and every English region played their part, then in a month we'd have nearly 10,000 more places for vulnerable refugees fleeing danger, seeking safety. Ten thousand instead of 200. [...]

We need to be able to look our grandparents in the eyes and say we faced up to the challenges and responsibilities of our time just as they did theirs. And we need to be able to look our grandchildren in the eyes and say we did not turn our backs. ... In the recession of the 1930s, Britain didn't just open its hearts to the 10,000 children of the Kindertransport, but our homes. It is that strength of compassion that makes Britain great.

So that is why today I am asking the Home Secretary to change policy. I'm asking the Prime Minister to show leadership and pledging my support if he does. I'm asking Parliament to back him. I'm asking Scotland and Wales to agree. I'm asking councils to offer places. I'm asking communities to offer help. I'm asking faith groups and charities to show the way. I'm asking campaigning organizations to mobilize support. I'm asking everyone to do their bit, however large or small.

The truth is I'm not really asking very much at all. I'm asking us to do something we've done before. Something we will do again. To help those who need us.

I'm asking Britain to be Britain.

MICHELLE OBAMA

'When They Go Low, We Go High'

DEMOCRATIC NATIONAL CONVENTION, PHILADELPHIA

July 2016

Barack Obama's presidency will be remembered for eloquent, authentic oratory. Much of it was delivered by the President, but the speeches by Michelle as First Lady were sometimes even more powerful.

Her speeches always came across as immensely personal and natural. She speaks with a wonderful combination of grace, compassion and authority, and looks as relaxed making speeches as chatting in person or talking to friends and family. Unusually, she's someone who manages to come across as very warm, and incredibly cool all at the same time – and all that comes across in her oratory too.

Recalling the beginning of their presidency in this speech during the 2016 presidential election campaign, she told us about their daughters, but then talked about the future for everyone's daughters and sons. She moved effortlessly between the personal and political. There is a moment in the narrative when the story of 'self', the story of their family, transforms into the story of 'us', the story of the nation. It is incredibly powerful.

> That is the story of this country. The story that has brought me to the stage tonight. The story of generations of people who felt the lash of bondage, the shame of servitude, the sting of segregation, who kept on striving, and hoping, and doing what needed to be done. So that today, I wake up every morning in a house that was built by slaves. And I watch my daughters, two beautiful, intelligent, black young women, play with the dog on the White House lawn.

The Obama speechwriters tried to achieve that kind of personal and political storytelling throughout their time in the White House – in this case it was Michelle Obama's very personal and heartfelt delivery that made it so moving.

But it can't have been easy for the family. Many of us in much less exposed positions in politics have had to think long and hard about how to protect our children. Ed and I tried always to keep our children out of photos and avoided telling their stories even when it felt much more human and natural to talk about them. But when you are the first family of the United States of America, you don't get that privacy and you don't get that choice. So both Barack and Michelle Obama had a difficult line to tread – drawing on their family experiences to tell powerful stories, yet with grace and dignity, keeping some private space for their daughters growing up too.

That dignity – so strong in Michelle Obama's speech and delivery – was in stark contrast to the mood of the divisive 2016 Clinton-Trump presidential election campaign, full of vitriol and venom. Political debate had become debased, full of Twitter spats and personal insults, and there couldn't have been a more timely retort than this speech.

Michelle Obama's support for Hillary Clinton is explicit and strong. And she delivers a clear and cutting critique of a Trump presidency without ever mentioning him by name. By this point in the campaign, crowds at Trump rallies were regularly calling for Hillary Clinton to be locked up or strung up, and the misogyny was shocking.

This speech was a strong moral response to the debasing of politics but it was also a wider call for decency in democracy – and one that far outlasts the 2016 presidential campaign. At a time when politics in many countries and online seems to be becoming more polarized, more vitriolic and abusive, Michelle Obama's words are a lesson in how to restore decency and grace into our politics.

As she said in her most memorable line:

When they go low, we go high.

It is hard to believe that it has been eight years since I first came to this convention to talk with you about why I thought my husband should be president. Remember how I told you about his character and his conviction? His decency and grace? The traits we have seen every day as he has served our country in the White House.

I also told you about our daughters, how they are the heart of our hearts, the centre of our world, and during our time in the White House we have had the joy of watching them grow from bubbly little girls into poised young women. A journey that started soon after we arrived in Washington when they set off for their first day at their new school.

I will never forget that winter morning as I watched our girls, just seven and ten years old, pile into those black SUVs with all those big men with guns. And I saw their little faces pressed up against the window, and the only thing I could think was, 'What have we done?'

At that moment, I realized that our time in the White House would form the foundation of who they would become. And how well we managed this experience could truly make or break them. That is what Barack and I think about every day as he tried to guide and protect our girls from the challenges of this unusual life in the spotlight.

How we urged them to ignore those who question their father's citizenship or faith.

How we insist that the hateful language they hear from public figures on TV does not represent the true spirit of this country.

How we explain that when someone is cruel or acts like a bully, you don't stoop to their level.

Our motto is: when they go low, we go high.

With every word we utter, with every action we take, we know our kids are watching us. We as parents are their most important role models.

Let me tell you, Barack and I take that same approach to our jobs as President and First Lady because we know that our words and actions matter, not just to our girls but the children across this country.

Kids who say, 'I saw you on TV', 'I wrote a report on you for school'.

Kids like the little black boy who looked up at my husband, his eyes wide with hope, and he wondered, 'Is my hair like yours?'

Make no mistake about it, this November, when we get to the polls, that is what we are deciding. Not Democrat or Republican, not left or right. In this election, and every election, it is about who will have the power to shape our children for the next four or eight years of their lives.

I am here tonight because in this election, there is only one person who I trust with that responsibility, only one person who I believe is truly qualified to be President of the United States, and that is our friend Hillary Clinton.

I trust Hillary to lead this country because I have seen her lifelong devotion to our nation's children. Not just her own daughter, who she has raised to perfection, but every child who needs a champion: kids who take the long way to school to avoid the gangs. Kids who wonder how they will ever afford college. Kids whose parents don't speak a word of English, but dream of a better life; who look to us to dream of what they can be.

Hillary has spent decades doing the relentless work to actually make a difference in their lives. Advocating for kids with disabilities as a young lawyer, fighting for children's healthcare as First Lady, and for quality childcare in the senate.

And when she did not win the nomination eight years ago, she did not get angry or disillusioned. Hillary did not pack up and go home, because as a true public servant Hillary knows that this is so much bigger than her own disappointment.

She proudly stepped up to serve our country once again as Secretary of State, travelling the globe to keep our kids safe. There were moments when Hillary could have decided that this work was too hard, that the price of public service was too high, that she was tired of being picked apart for how she looked, or how she talked, or even how she laughed.

But here's the thing: what I admire most about Hillary is that she never buckles under pressure. She never takes the easy way out. And Hillary Clinton has never quit on anything in her life.

And when I think about the kind of president that I want for my girls and all our children, that is what I want. I want someone with the proven strength to persevere. Somebody who knows this job and takes it seriously. Somebody who understands that the issues of our nation are not black or white and cannot be boiled down to 140 characters. Because when you have the nuclear codes at your fingertips and the military in your command, you can't make snap decisions. You can't have thin skin or a tendency to lash out. You need to be steady and measured and well informed.

I want a president with a record of public service. Someone whose life's work shows our children that we don't chase fame and fortune for ourselves; we fight to give everyone a chance to succeed. And we give back even when we are struggling ourselves because we know that there is always someone worse off. And there but for the grace of God, go I.

I want a president who will teach our children that everyone in this country matters. A president who truly believes what our founders put forth all those years ago: that we are all created equal, each a beloved part of the great American story. When crisis hits, we don't turn against each other, we listen to each other. We lean on each other. We are always stronger together.

I am here tonight because I know that that is the kind of president Hillary Clinton will be and that is why in this election, I'm with her.

You see, Hillary understands that the presidency is about one thing and one thing only. It is about leaving something better for our kids. That is how we have always moved this country forward; by all of us coming together on behalf of our children. Folks who volunteer to coach the team, teach the Sunday school class, because they know it takes a village.

Heroes of every colour and creed who wear the uniform and risk their lives to pass on those blessings of liberty; police officers and protesters in Dallas who all desperately want to keep our children safe; people who lined up in Orlando to donate blood because it could have been their son, or their daughter in that club. [...]

Leaders like Hillary Clinton, who have the guts and the grace to keep coming back and putting those cracks in the highest and hardest glass ceiling until she finally breaks through, lifting all of us along with her.

That is the story of this country. The story that has brought me to the stage tonight. The story of generations of people who felt the lash of bondage, the shame of servitude, the sting of segregation, who kept on striving, and hoping, and doing what needed to be done. So that today, I wake up every morning in a house that was built by slaves. And

I watch my daughters, two beautiful, intelligent, black young women, play with their dog on the White House lawn.

And because of Hillary Clinton, my daughters and all our sons and daughters now take for granted that a woman can be President of the United States.

So don't let anyone ever tell you that this country is not great. That somehow we need to make it great again. Because this right now is the greatest country on earth.

And as my daughters set out in the world, I want a leader who is worthy of that truth, a leader worthy of my girls' promise and all of our kids' promise. A leader who will be guided every day by the love and hope and impossibly big dreams that we all have for our children.

In this election, we cannot sit back and hope that everything works out for the best; we cannot afford to be tired or frustrated or cynical.

Hear me: between now and November, we need to do what we did eight years ago and four years ago. We need to knock on every door, we need to get out every vote, we need to pour every last ounce of passion into electing Hillary Clinton as President of the United States of America. Let's get to work.

DONNA STRICKLAND

'Physics Is Fun'

NOBEL BANQUET, STOCKHOLM

December 2018

Donna Strickland's excitement about experimental physics is infectious. Thirty years after her graduate student breakthrough on the power of lasers, she and the team she had worked with were awarded the Nobel Prize for Physics. It was only the third time ever that a woman had been awarded the prize – and the first for fifty-five years.

So Strickland used her moment in the Nobel limelight brilliantly. This speech bubbles with energy and passion – for the wonder of lasers, the fun of solving puzzles, building new toys and the sheer magic of discovery. It is a deliberate and effective attempt to convey the fun of physics and to inspire others to follow her path.

She doesn't talk about the huge impact of her work on the world, how she developed ways to intensify the power of lasers, which transformed medical procedures like laser eye surgery. Instead she describes the enjoyment of the journey – staying late in the lab, solving problem after problem, machining endless parts and finally creating something entirely new. Even just reading these words, you can feel how exhilarating that moment was for her.

Since she was awarded her Nobel Prize, she says she has heard from so many young women and girls who say they feel inspired to pursue science education or careers in STEM fields.

I loved the puzzles of physics at school – it did feel like trying to uncover the magic forces that held the world together. But I was one of just a small handful of girls in a class of boys choosing to study it at my comprehensive school and sixth form in the 1980s – and it was easy to get put off or feel like an outsider. Thirty years on, my daughter had a similar experience.

So it's brilliant that Strickland has become a role model for young girls around the world at a time when women are under-represented in STEM fields, and girls make up only 20 per cent of A level physics students in the UK[33] and 20 per cent of physics undergraduates in the US.[34]

Astonishingly, 97 per cent of Nobel Prize winners for science have been men.[35] Hopefully Donna Strickland's pioneering work and enthusiasm will change that and help others feel the fun.

It is my honour to represent the Nobel Prize in Physics 2018 and speak on behalf of Arthur Ashkin and Gérard Mourou, my esteemed colleagues with whom I share the prize. […]

As has been pointed out, I join Marie Curie and Maria Goeppert Mayer as the only women to win this prize. I am humbled to be in their company. Marie Curie is in a class all her own as the first female winner and still the only person to win the Nobel Prize in two different science categories. An astounding scientist.

For her PhD, Maria Goeppert Mayer, a theoretical physicist, came up with the idea of multi-photon physics. That means an atom absorbs two or more photons simultaneously. She made the prediction without any experimental evidence and in fact it would be another thirty years before anyone observed the effect. I cited her theory in my PhD thesis more than fifty years later.

And as for me – when I was in grad school, working on the project for which Gérard and I are being honoured, Cyndi Lauper had a big hit: 'Girls Just Want to Have Fun'. But they wanted to wait until the working day is done. As for me, I want to have fun while I'm working. Now not everyone thinks physics is fun, but I do. I think experimental physics is especially fun, because not only do you get to solve puzzles about the universe or here on earth, there are really cool toys in the lab. In my case, I get to play with high intensity lasers that can do magical things, like take one colour of laser light and turn it into a rainbow of colours. Just one of the amazing things we get to see in our laser labs.

Gérard Mourou, who was my PhD supervisor, dreamed up the idea of increasing laser intensity by orders of magnitude. He did it while he was on a ski trip with his family. He probably shouldn't have been thinking about lasers. He just couldn't help himself. It was my job to take Gérard's beautiful idea and make it a reality. I built a pulse stretcher, then a laser amplifier and then finally a pulse compressor. To do so, I had to learn to cleave optical fibre, machine a lot of parts, do a lot of plumbing. Are you feeling the fun? I had to measure the pulse durations and the frequency spectrum. Not all of the measurements showed what we expected. We had to figure out the problems and then a way around them. That was the fun part.

That all took about a year. Then it was finally time to measure the duration of the compressed, amplified pulses and I had no way to measure it. Steve Williamson, my colleague, had the way and he wheeled his streak camera into my lab one night, and together we measured the compressed pulse width of the amplified pulses. I will never forget that night. It is truly an amazing feeling when you know that you have built something that no one else ever has – and it actually works.

There really is no excitement quite like it … except for maybe getting woken up at five in the morning because the Royal Swedish Academy of Sciences [and the Nobel Foundation] also think it was an exciting moment for the field of laser physics.

So on behalf of Arthur Ashkin, Gérard Mourou and me, thank you to the Royal Swedish Academy of Sciences and the Nobel Foundation for honouring us and laser physics with this Nobel Prize.

ALEXANDRIA OCASIO-CORTEZ

'Today I Rise'

UNITED STATES CONGRESS
January 2019

In the November 2018 midterm elections in the US, more women stood as candidates than ever before. One of them was Alexandria Ocasio-Cortez.

A year before, AOC – as she's now known – was working eighteen-hour shifts in a Mexican restaurant in her neighbourhood. Now she is the youngest ever member of Congress.

Already, she has electrified US politics. She won the primary to become a Democrat candidate against the odds and has deliberately defied convention and shaken up tradition ever since. She takes her Instagram followers with her from Capitol Hill to her allotment and back to her apartment where she live-streams cooking dinner while answering political questions. When right-wing opponents tried to discredit her with a video of her dancing in high school, she uploaded a video dancing in her Congress office.

Her speeches and committee appearances are compelling. She is a brilliant and refreshing storyteller; she makes problems come alive, and injustices ache. In her congressional committee sessions, she is creative and clever.

This speech is her first in Congress after being elected. It's about the 2019 New Year stand-off between President Trump and Congress over the border wall which shut down federal government.

Only AOC doesn't start with a stand-off, a wall, a political attack or a constitutional conflict. Instead she tells us the story of one of her constituents, Mr Obed, a man who hasn't had a pay cheque for weeks but is working without wages to keep planes safely in the sky. The simple story of the air traffic controller brings home how much is at stake and how shocking and irresponsible the government shutdown is.

Then she builds her argument about the responsibility of the president with a repeated refrain – 'it is not normal' to stop people's pay cheques, to treat air traffic controllers like this, to treat Mr Obed like this. It is a clear message, powerfully conveyed.

But perhaps the most significant line is the first one. Having campaigned to get into Congress as an underdog, not yet thirty years old, from the Bronx, knowing the expectations on her shoulders from the millions excited and energized by her bold campaign, this was her first chance to find her voice in the most powerful legislature in the world.

A sign of more to come, she begins, 'Today, I rise'.

Today I rise to tell the story of one of my constituents, Yahi Obed. Mr Obed was born in Yemen and came to the United States when he was eight years old. His childhood dream was to become a pilot, and he knew and felt that in the United States all things were possible and that his dream could come true.

Mr Obed's dream did come true. He has been a federal employee for fourteen years, has two children and a mortgage for his home in the Morris Park neighbourhood of the Bronx. He studied hard, got his pilot's licence, and is now an air traffic controller supervisor at John F. Kennedy International Airport in New York City. I spoke with Mr Obed today over the phone, he and air traffic controllers like him across the country missed their first pay cheque this past week.

He was telling me about how stressful his job is: every single day air traffic controllers have thousands of people's lives in their hands. With weather changes, flight delays, staffing complexities and a myriad of other issues, their days almost never go exactly to plan. His job is to find solutions, analyse and adapt in real time to keep people safe in one of the busiest airspaces in the US and the world.

And it is terrifying to think that almost every single air traffic controller in the US is currently distracted at work because they don't know when their next pay cheque is coming.

Federal workers' jobs are stressful enough. The rise in New York City's cost of living is stressful enough. The fact that Mr Obed's family cannot be reunified due to fears over the Muslim ban is stressful enough. His several-thousand-dollar-a-month Bronx mortgage is stressful enough. The anti-immigrant sentiment of this administration is stressful enough.

And the truth of this shutdown is that it's actually not about a wall, it is not about the border, and it is certainly not about the well-being of everyday Americans. The truth is, this shutdown is about the erosion of American democracy and the subversion of our most basic governmental norms.

It is not normal to hold 800,000 workers' pay cheques hostage.

It is not normal to shut down the government when we don't get what we want.

It is not normal for public servants to run away and hide from the public that they serve.

It is certainly not normal to starve the people we serve for a proposal that is wildly unpopular among the American people.

Each and every member of this body has a responsibility to this nation and to everyone in the United States of America, whether they voted for us or not, and this President shares in that responsibility as well, which means he has a responsibility to my constituent, Mr Obed.

President Trump has a responsibility to all air traffic controllers, FDA inspectors, TSA workers, and he has a responsibility to maintain the basic functioning of the United States government.

Thank you very much, Madam Speaker, I yield my time.

JACINDA ARDERN

'They Are Us'

CHRISTCHURCH

March 2019

Jacinda Ardern's response to the awful terrorist attack in Christchurch was a lesson in compassionate and determined leadership.

On 15 March 2019, fifty-one people were killed in two mosques in Christchurch, on New Zealand's South Island. The terrible events were live-streamed by the attacker on Facebook and haunting images were plastered across social media and news sites around the world.

The attacker's intention was to spread terror and hate towards the Muslim community in New Zealand, but the response was an outpouring of love and solidarity with them. Jacinda Ardern's extraordinary empathy and immediate leadership in response to the attack set the tone. Non-Muslim women across the country wore headscarves to show their respect; the Muslim call to prayer was broadcast on national TV and radio; groups of school students performed the haka to express their solidarity; and New Zealanders from across the country attended candlelit vigils in their tens of thousands.

The rest of us watched, moved at how this country had come together in the face of unspeakable violence and loss.

This speech, given at a memorial service two weeks later, sets an example for every political leader who is faced with a grieving nation, and who, in the aftermath of violence that is intended to divide a nation, has the task of bringing it together as one.

From the day of the attack to this moment a fortnight later, Ardern's message was clear. The victims and their community are us. The attacker – his views and his violence – is not. In an address to Parliament after the attack, Ardern said resolutely: 'You won't hear me speak his name.' She didn't dictate that anyone else – the media or otherwise – must follow that rule, but in making her own moral stand, she led the way for others to follow.

In this speech, Ardern spoke about a nation not having had the right words to adequately describe its pain, but then finding them with those who were grieving the most: *As-salaam Alaikum*. Peace be upon you.

Dressed in a traditional Maori cloak, Ardern infused phrases of indigenous Maori with phrases of Arabic and with English. And just by using those three languages together in this address – effortlessly moving from one to the other – she was unifying New Zealand, and I think she was healing it too.

By sharing every moment of suffering with the Muslim community, using their words, sharing their tears, respecting their dress, she didn't distinguish their pain from the pain of the country as a whole. Her ending of the speech illustrates that so powerfully. First in Maori: *Ko tātou tatou* (We are one). And then in Arabic: *As-salaam Alaikum* (Peace be upon you).

Imam Gamal Fouda of Al Noor Mosque, where one of the shootings took place, gave thanks to Ardern after she'd given her speech:

> Thank you for your leadership, it has been a lesson for the world's leaders. Thank you for your words and tears of compassion. Thank you for being one with us.

Ardern's response wasn't just compassionate, it was swift and firm – calling out social media companies who facilitated the proliferation of this extremist poison, and reforming gun laws, immediately and unapologetically.

Within one week of the Christchurch attack Ardern announced a sweeping ban on assault rifles and military-style semi-automatics, as well as high-capacity magazines and any parts that convert guns into semi-automatic weapons. Announcing the measures, she said: 'In short, every semi-automatic weapon used in the terrorist attack on Friday will be banned in this country.'

We shouldn't underestimate the importance of the way Jacinda Ardern responded to Christchurch. It is easy for communities to become angrier, more divided, more hostile to each other, more susceptible to conspiracy theories, more brittle when appalling attacks like this happen. That's what the terrorists want. Bad leaders fail to understand that, or at worst end up escalating and exploiting it. Ardern, in her speech and response, showed true leadership for both New Zealand and the world.

E rau rangatira mā, e ngā reo, e ngā mana. Tēnā koutou katoa.

(I acknowledge amongst us today our distinguished leaders, speakers and those who bear authority.)

Ngāi Tahu Whānui, tēnā koutou.

(My greetings to the whole of Ngāi Tahu.)

E papaki tū ana ngā tai o maumahara ki runga o Ōtautahi.

(The tides of remembrance flow over Christchurch today.)

Haere mai tātou me te aroha, me te rangimārie, ki te whānau nei, e ora mārire ai anō rātau, e ora mārire ai anō, tātou katoa.

(So let us gather with love, in peace, for this family, so that they may truly live again, so that we all may truly live again.)

We gather here, fourteen days on from our darkest of hours. In the days that have followed the terrorist attack on the fifteenth of March, we have often found ourselves without words.

What words adequately express the pain and suffering of fifty men, women and children lost, and so many injured? What words capture the anguish of our Muslim community being the target of hatred and violence? What words express the grief of a city that has already known so much pain?

I thought there were none. And then I came here and was met with this simple greeting. *As-salaam Alaikum.* Peace be upon you.

They were simple words, repeated by community leaders who witnessed the loss of their friends and loved ones.

Simple words, whispered by the injured from their hospital beds.

Simple words, spoken by the bereaved and everyone I met who has been affected by this attack.

As-salaam Alaikum. Peace be upon you.

They were words spoken by a community who, in the face of hate and violence, had every right to express anger but instead opened their doors for all of us to grieve with them. And so we say to those who have lost the most, we may not have always had the words. We may have left flowers, performed the haka, sung songs or simply embraced. But even when we had no words, we still heard yours, and they have left us humbled and they have left us united.

Over the past two weeks we have heard the stories of those impacted by this terrorist attack. They were stories of bravery. They were stories of those who were born here, grew up here, or who had made New Zealand their home. Who had sought refuge, or sought a better life for themselves or their families.

These stories, they now form part of our collective memories. They will remain with us forever. They are us.

But with that memory comes a responsibility. A responsibility to be the place that we wish to be. A place that is diverse, that is welcoming, that is kind and compassionate. Those values represent the very best of us.

But even the ugliest of viruses can exist in places they are not welcome. Racism exists, but it is not welcome here. An assault on the freedom of any one of us who practises their faith or religion, is not welcome here. Violence, and extremism in all its forms, is not welcome here. And over the last two weeks we have shown that, you have shown that, in your actions.

From the thousands at vigils to the 95-year-old man who took four buses to attend a rally because he couldn't sleep from the sadness of seeing the hurt and suffering of others. Our challenge now is to make the very best of us a daily reality. Because we are not immune to the viruses of hate, of fear, of other. We never have been. But we can be the nation that discovers the cure.

And so to each of us as we go from here, we have work to do, but do not leave the job of combatting hate to the government alone. We each hold the power, in our words and in our actions, in our daily acts of kindness. Let that be the legacy of the fifteenth of March. To be the nation we believe ourselves to be.

To the global community who have joined us today, who reached out to embrace New Zealand, and our Muslim community, to all of those who have gathered here with us, we say thank you.

And we also ask that the condemnation of violence and terrorism turns now to a collective response. The world has been stuck in a vicious cycle of extremism breeding extremism and it must end.

We cannot confront these issues alone, none of us can. But the answer to them lies in a simple concept that is not bound by domestic borders, that isn't based on ethnicity, power base or even forms of governance. The answer lies in our humanity.

But for now, we will remember those who have left this place. We will remember the first responders who gave so much of themselves to save others. We will remember the tears of our nation, and the new resolve we have formed.

And we remember that ours is a home that does not and cannot claim perfection. But we can strive to be true to the words embedded in our national anthem:
Men of every creed and race,
Gather here before Thy face,
Asking Thee to bless this place,
God defend our free land.
From dissension, envy, hate
And corruption, guard our state,
Make our country good and great,
God defend New Zealand.

Ko tātou tātou.

As-salaam Alaikum.

DIANE ABBOTT

'We Will Not Rest'

HOUSE OF COMMONS

April 2019

When Diane Abbott was elected to the British House of Commons in 1987, she was the first – and for ten years the only – black woman MP, and, along with Bernie Grant and Paul Boateng, that year she was one of the first three black MPs ever elected.

Diane is a trailblazer, and she has been a passionate campaigner for over thirty years in public life, challenging governments of all parties when they fail to treat people with dignity and respect.

In her maiden speech in the House of Commons thirty years ago, she spoke about her Jamaican parents and others like them from across the Commonwealth who had come to Britain in the 1950s for a better life. She said:

> A whole generation of black and ethnic minority immigrants came – not to sponge, not to swamp anyone else's culture, not to provide objects of derision for Conservative Members, but to work. They came for a better life for their children. They also came with pride, as citizens of Britain and its Commonwealth, and believing in that citizenship.

She went on to warn against both the Conservative government's new immigration legislation being debated in Parliament that day, and against rising anti-immigration sentiment in the country.

The generation of immigrants Diane talked so powerfully about in that speech was often referred to as the Windrush generation, named after the ship on which so many families sailed from the Caribbean to help rebuild Britain's economy and country after the war. And Diane's words about their pride, hard work and citizenship, spoken thirty years ago, would be echoed in the spring of 2019 as Diane stood up to make the speech I've included here on the Windrush scandal, which revealed that hundreds of people from the Windrush generation had been wrongly detained and deported by the Home Office.

The speech is a response to a government statement in the House of Commons, so it is short, and is peppered with questions directed at the Home Secretary. But it is testament to Diane's skill as a speaker that her words nonetheless encapsulate with authority the depth of the injustice done to the Windrush generation, as well as its roots in many years of British government policy.

Diane has also had to be far more resilient and determined than any MP should ever have to be. The abuse and threats targeted at her have been greater than those against any other MP – vile racism as well as misogyny on social media, in emails, letters and at public events. Research by Amnesty International found that Diane received almost half of all the abusive tweets sent to female MPs in the run-up to the 2017 general election, ten times more than any other MP.[36] This is deliberate and organized racism and misogyny, it corrodes democracy and no one should have to put up with it.

Like many women MPs facing threats and abuse, Diane has spent many years dealing with it and getting on with the job. But she has also spoken out and challenged social media companies to act to prevent this torrent of abuse. In her own words:

> The people who go online to abuse women and black people, they want to drive us out of the public space and ultimately they want to destroy us as people.[37]

Diane has never been driven out or silenced by the abuse she receives. She has continued to be a bold advocate for others – as an MP for Hackney North and Stoke Newington for over thirty years, as a shadow minister, and now as Shadow Home Secretary. But as she has rightly warned:

> This is not just about politicians, it's not even about just women politicians, any woman that goes into the public space can expect this type of abuse … it is about the degradation of public discourse.[38]

All of us have a responsibility to drive out vitriolic and violent language from our public life. As Diane makes clear – this is about the protection of democracy itself.

We have to remember in this House how much pride the Windrush generation took in being British. We have to remember that they came here in good faith under passports which indicated to them that they were indeed British. There are all the material challenges they faced as part of the Windrush scandal but, above all, having spoken to numbers of these people, there was the humiliation of being told year on year by the British state that somehow they were not British, they were not worthy, they were not deserving and services they had paid into for years and years were not available to them.

The reality is that this is a scandal that should never have happened. It is a scandal to which the government were initially slow to react and it is a scandal in which some Members of Parliament deliberately muddied the waters with talk of illegal immigrants, when, by definition, none of the Windrush victims is here illegally. It is a scandal that is set to continue unless and until the government end their hostile environment. […]

The Prime Minister told us that she would fight 'burning injustices'. Well, the Windrush scandal was a burning injustice and it took place on her watch, first as Home Secretary and then as Prime Minister. Her successor as Home Secretary [Amber Rudd] was obliged to relinquish her post because she incorrectly told the House that there were no numerical deportation targets. We have since learned that the Right Hon. Member for Hastings and Rye [Amber Rudd] had written to the Prime Minister promising to increase deportations by 10 per cent. We also know that deportation numbers were a key performance indicator when she presided over home affairs, and that Home Office officials received bonuses relating to the numbers of deportees.

It is hard to imagine that these targets, performance indicators and bonuses did not affect the lack of care with which the Windrush generation were treated. The current Home Secretary told the House in April last year: 'I will do whatever it takes to put it right.' He also said: 'We have made it clear that a Commonwealth citizen who has remained in the UK since 1973 will be eligible to get the legal status that they deserve: British citizenship.'

And yet here we are.

We know that many citizens from the Commonwealth who have been here since 1973 have still not been granted British citizenship and are still not treated as British citizens. […]

We welcome the fact that the Home Secretary accepts that this is not just about persons from the Caribbean. The Windrush generation is so called because of that emblematic symbol, the *Empire Windrush*, but it actually involves anyone from a Commonwealth country who came to this country between 1948 and 1972. I believe that many more persons will need to come forward if we are really going to clear up this scandal.

Will the Home Secretary say a little about the hardship fund, which was set up in response to pressure … to deal with the immediate issues faced by the Windrush generation? … Is it true that thus far only two people have had payments from the fund? … Is he willing to comment on the fact that the scheme will not compensate those who may have gone back to the Caribbean or elsewhere in the Commonwealth for a holiday or a funeral and who were not allowed to get back on the plane? The document states that it is difficult to ascertain 'whether inability to return to the UK is a loss'.

Of course it is a loss. That is an extraordinary thing to say. We know that people were wrongly prevented from returning to their home here. The Home Secretary admits that. One of the reasons was that they were unable to provide documentary proof of their status. Now the Home Secretary proposes to exclude them from compensation. These people were British citizens, yet they were unable to return to their home here and in some cases they were separated from their families. This is not ending the scandal; it continues it. [...]

Let me say finally that there are some in this House who are the children of the Windrush generation. Whether we are on the frontbenches or the backbenches, and whether we are in opposition or in government, we will not rest until that generation, one of the bravest generations, gets the justice to which it is entitled.

LILIT MARTIROSYAN

'We Are Making History Today'

Few national parliaments anywhere in the world have heard speeches from transgender women. So when Lilit Martirosyan spoke in the Armenian Parliament in April 2019 she was blazing a brave trail across the world, not just in Armenia, shining a light on the violence, crimes and discrimination experienced by transgender people everywhere. But that makes the violent response she received even more deeply disturbing.

Martirosyan's speech was short and very simple. She did not ask much of the Armenian representatives – calling on them simply to be involved in legislation on gender equality and human rights in general. Instead the main focus and purpose of the speech was descriptive – to speak truth to power about the terrible violence and crime she and other transgender Armenians experience.

> People like myself have been tortured, raped, kidnapped, subjected to physical violence, burned, immolated, knifed, subjected to attempted murder, emigrated, robbed, subjected to stigma and discrimination in social, medical, legal, economic areas and in every aspect of a dignified life.

As founder of the transgender rights organization Right Side in Armenia and the first registered transgender woman in the country, Martirosyan has been a formidable activist at home. But she wasn't just speaking for Armenia. Even in countries with the longest history of LGBT+ rights, transphobia is widespread, often including appalling violence. Speaking in 2014 at a Creating Change conference in the US, actress and LGBT+ advocate Laverne Cox said: 'Some days, I wake up and I have heard about another one of my transgender sisters who has been assaulted, raped, murdered... And there is no justice.'[39] Here in the UK in 2018, recorded hate crime against the transgender community went up by 81 per cent.[40]

Disturbingly, the response to Martirosyan's speech proved her point in the worst of ways. A parliamentarian called for her to be burned alive. An anti-LGBT+ demonstration amassed outside the Parliament building to protest her right to speak; one of them brought a knife and announced that he wanted to kill her.[41] Martirosyan's home address was leaked online, and so were the addresses of her Right Side colleagues and family members. She spent the following weeks in hiding.[42]

Same-sex relationships were decriminalized in Armenia in 2003, and many thought the peaceful revolution of 2018 would be the dawn of a more tolerant kind of politics.[43] But Martirosyan had shown that simply by being visible, and simply by describing the violence she and others had experienced, she became the target of further violence, hatred and abuse.

Lilit Martirosyan exposed the considerable bravery of trans women and trans men across the world for simply living their lives true to themselves. But she also showed great bravery herself in speaking out and giving the voiceless a voice. And she's shown the importance for the rest of us in speaking out in solidarity against transphobia and homophobia across the world.

Dear Members of Parliament, colleagues and guests, we are making history today.

Even a few months ago, it was impossible to even imagine what is today a reality in the post-Revolution Armenia. I am delivering this speech to you from Armenian Parliament's tribune, as a transgender woman.

But I ask you to see me as a collective figure, being a member of the Armenian transgender community, and the president of the 'Right Side' human rights NGO; people like myself have been tortured, raped, kidnapped, subjected to physical violence, burned, immolated, knifed, subjected to attempted murder, emigrated, robbed, subjected to stigma and discrimination in social, medical, legal, economic areas and in every aspect of a dignified life, unemployed, poor and morally abandoned.

Up until 2018, we have registered 283 similar cases against transgender people and I don't know what is scarier – this number, or the fact that only a minor part of these cases were registered by the police or by other competent bodies. And if you take '283' as the number of transgender people in Armenia whose rights were violated, then, for me, it means that there are 283 criminals in Armenia living next to me and you. And who knows, maybe the 284th will commit their crime just tomorrow.

What is also concerning is that people who defend transgender people are also subjected to physical violence and persecution.

In just one month, some people cut the throat of one transgender person, violently beat another in their own apartment, and completely burned down the apartment, including their personal belongings.

Think about this, gentlemen. I call upon you, including the representatives of transgender people, to get involved in the implementation of policies and legislative reforms related to gender equality and ensuring human rights in general.

We are ready to support you in building democracy in our homeland.

Thank you.

GRETA THUNBERG

'Let's Start Acting'

R20 AUSTRIAN WORLD SUMMIT, VIENNA

May 2019

No one speaks about the future with more clarity or urgency than Greta Thunberg.

The Swedish sixteen-year-old with signature pigtails has taken the world by storm since she skipped school in August 2018 to protest about the climate emergency outside the Swedish Parliament. She started a tidal wave of youth activism on the climate crisis, which culminated in more than a million students from around the world taking part in school strikes this spring.

Greta Thunberg has become their champion. The voice of a new generation.

In some ways she is an unlikely figurehead – she's a teenager from Sweden, for whom English is only a second language, and she has talked publicly and bravely about having Asperger's syndrome, a form of autism. But none of that has held her back. On the contrary, she insists that her activism is successful because of her autism, not in spite of it. She told the BBC, 'being different is a gift… It makes me see things from outside the box. I don't easily fall for lies, I can see through things.'[44]

That is evident in her speeches. They are refreshingly direct.

When she came to the British Parliament to address MPs in April 2019, she asked:

'Is the microphone really on?'

[Yes]

'Did you hear me?'

[Yes]

'Is my English OK?'

[Yes]

'Because I'm beginning to wonder.'[45]

Within a week of her visit to Parliament, followed by a wave of disruptive climate protests by campaign group Extinction Rebellion, MPs voted for the first time to declare a climate emergency.[46]

It wasn't a coincidence.

Greta's speeches are effective because they shame the inaction of those with power. She tells off the grown-ups in the room; she exposes their recklessness and their irresponsibility. Her words in this speech to distinguished guests in Vienna are angry and alarmist. The audience doesn't get off lightly with the polite pleasantries typically afforded to politicians and CEOs. Her speech to the United Nations a few months later was even more stark.

Every time she speaks she is sounding an alarm bell and forcing people to listen, forcing them to act. Her words are a challenge to leaders but also a rallying cry to others to join her:

…we will not let you get away with it anymore.

The impact of Thunberg's campaigning and her blunt, urgent style of speaking have been truly remarkable. Climate scientists who have been trying for decades to be heard say this teenager has made people finally start to listen. Greta Thunberg is displaying the leadership that she calls for from others. Like all the women in this compilation and millions of others around the world, Greta Thunberg is using her voice to demand action and ultimately to inspire hope for the future.

Thank you for inviting me, and thank you for having me here, and thank you everyone for coming.

My name is Greta Thunberg. I am a climate activist from Sweden. And for the last nine months, I have been school striking for the climate every Friday in front of the Swedish Parliament.

We need to change the way we treat the climate crisis. We need to change the way we speak about the climate crisis. And we need to call it what it is: an emergency.

I am certain that most of us in here today are generally aware of the situation. But my number one experience during these last nine months is that people in general have no clue. Many of us know something is wrong, that the planet is warming because of increased greenhouse gases, but we don't know the exact consequences of that. The vast majority know much less than we think. And this should be no surprise.

We have never been shown the graphs which show how much the CO_2 emissions need to be reduced for us to stay below the 1.5°C limit. We have never been told the meaning of the aspect of equity in the Paris agreements and why it's so important. We have never been taught about feedback loops, or tipping points, or what a runaway greenhouse effect is. Most of us don't know almost any of the basic facts.

Because how could we? We have not been told. Or more importantly, we have never been told by the right people.

We are *Homo sapiens sapiens*, of the family *Hominidae*, of the order *Primates*, of the class *Mammalia*, of the kingdom *Animalia*. We are a part of nature. We are social animals. We are naturally drawn to our leaders.

During the last months, millions of children have been school striking for the climate, gaining lots of attention for the climate crisis. But we children are not leaders. Nor are the scientists, unfortunately.

But many of you here today are. Presidents, celebrities, politicians, CEOs and journalists. People listen to you. They are influenced by you. And therefore you have an enormous responsibility. And let's be honest, this is a responsibility that most of you have failed to take.

You cannot rely on people reading between the lines or searching for the information themselves, to read through the latest IPCC report, track the Keeling Curve, or keep tabs on the world's rapidly disappearing carbon budgets. You have to explain that to us, repeatedly. No matter how uncomfortable or unprofitable that may be. And yes, a transformed world will include lots of new benefits. But you have to understand, this is not primarily an opportunity to create new green jobs, new businesses, or green economic growth. This is above all an emergency. And not just any emergency. This is the biggest crisis humanity has ever faced. This is not something you can 'like' on Facebook.

When I first heard about the climate and ecological breakdown, I actually didn't believe that this could be happening. Because how could it be? How could we be facing an existential crisis that will threaten our very survival, and yet that wasn't our first priority. If there really was a crisis this big, then we would rarely talk about anything else. As soon as you turned on the TV, almost everything would be about that. Headlines, radio, newspapers, you would almost never hear or read about anything else. And the politicians would surely have done what was needed by now, wouldn't they? They would hold crisis meetings all the time, declare climate emergencies everywhere, and spend all their waking hours handling this situation and informing the people what was going on.

But it never was like that. The climate crisis was just treated like any other issue, or even less than that. Every time you heard a politician speak about this, they never talked with urgency. According to them, there were always countless new technologies and simple solutions that, when put in place, would solve everything. Politicians one second say, 'climate change is very important, it is the most important topic, and we are going to do everything we can to stop it', and the next second they want to expand airports, build new coal power plants and motorways, and then they fly off in a private jet to attend a meeting on the other side of the world. That is not how you act in a crisis.

Humans are social animals. We can't get away from that fact. And as long as you, the leaders, act like everything is fine, and you have things under control, then us people won't understand that we are in an emergency.

You can't only keep talking about specific, isolated solutions to specific, isolated problems. We need to see the full picture. If you say that we can solve this crisis just by maybe increasing or lowering some taxes, phasing out coal in ten or fifteen years, putting up solar panels on new buildings, or manufacturing new electrical cars – if you say that, then people will think we can solve this crisis without anyone making a real effort.

And that is very dangerous because specific, isolated solutions are no longer enough. And you know this. We now need to change practically everything. We now need a whole new way of thinking.

I know you are desperate for hope and solutions. But the biggest source of hope and the easiest solution is right in front of you, and has been all along. And it is us people, and the fact that we don't know. We humans are not stupid. We are not ruining the biosphere and future living conditions for all species because we are evil. We are simply not aware. But once we understand, once we realize the situation, then we act. We change. Humans are very adaptable.

So instead of only being obsessed with finding solutions to a problem that most of us do not even know exists, you must also focus on informing us about the actual problem. We must acknowledge that we do not have all the solutions now. We must admit that we do not have the situation under control. And we must admit that we are losing this battle. We must stop playing with words and numbers, because we no longer have time for that. And in the words of author Alex Steffen, 'winning slowly is the same thing as losing', when it comes to the climate crisis.

The longer we wait, the harder it will be to turn this around. So let's not wait any longer. Let's start acting. For too long, the people in power have gotten away with basically not doing anything to stop the climate and ecological breakdown. They have gotten away with stealing our future and selling it for profit.

But we young people are waking up. And we promise we will not let you get away with it anymore.

Thank you.

MEGAN RAPINOE

'Be Better, Be Bigger'

NEW YORK

July 2019

Great coaches and team captains know how to make speeches. Although we rarely think of the pep talks before a match or at half time as 'speeches', these are the crucial words that inspire the team to come out fighting, these are demonstrations of leadership both on and off the pitch. Megan Rapinoe, co-captain of the USA women's football team, takes team talks to a new level.

In the 2019 Women's World Cup, Rapinoe became the international face of the tournament. She scored six goals, helped lead the USA to their fourth World Cup victory, and grabbed attention with her outspokenness and her signature statue-like celebration with her arms elegantly outstretched – before her teammates jumped in. According to Nike, the USA women's home shirt was the number one football jersey – men's or women's – ever sold on their website in one season.[47] I'm sure that was in no small part down to the profile and popularity of Megan Rapinoe.

Some male journalists branded her arrogant and dislikeable; I think she exemplified sporting power and poise. Few of those same commentators complain when Usain Bolt celebrates with his trademark lightning bolt pose or when Cristiano Ronaldo celebrates a goal with his familiar mid-air twist.

The 2019 World Cup was a breakthrough moment for women's football. FIFA reported that a record-breaking 1.12 billion viewers tuned in to watch the tournament in 2019, up from three-quarters of a million in 2015.[48] Formidable women athletes have been making waves for years, and it is brilliant to watch them doing so – Serena Williams winning Wimbledon after Wimbledon, Olympic athlete Jessica Ennis-Hill and Paralympic swimmer Ellie Simmonds winning gold medals in Beijing and London. But too often, impressive women have had to put up with double standards, lack of funding or encouragement, lower pay, sexist commentary and a myriad of other challenges.

In 2019, for the first time here in the UK, the Women's World Cup created an electric atmosphere. Pubs were full of people watching the games and singing 'Three Lions', and families and friends across the country gathered together to watch and support our Lionesses until they were knocked out by the USA in the semi-finals. Our family watched matches at home while I was finishing the first hardback edition of this book – and when I saw this speech by Rapinoe at a victory fan rally in New York just after the tournament, I wished I'd had the chance to include it.

I love the way that in this speech she pokes fun at all those who branded her arrogant – she jokes that she is too busy to run in the presidential race right now. Her opposition to President Trump, and her insistence during the tournament that she wouldn't go to the White House if invited, prompted an angry backlash from the President on Twitter, in which he accused her of disrespecting the country. And yet, intentionally or not, Rapinoe's message of compassion, community and coming together in the later part of this speech is more presidential than anything we've heard come out of the White House in the last few years.

Effortlessly calm and cool, surrounded by her teammates, Rapinoe delivered this speech with passion but also with purpose. She celebrates the team and those who support them behind the scenes, but her real message in this address is that whoever we are and whatever we do, we're all part of something bigger; we're all part of a community and we all have a part to play in making it kinder and more inclusive. This is her direct challenge to the fans watching. Building up our sense of defiance against those who might knock us down, enthusing us with camaraderie and then urging us to be better than we are – Rapinoe is delivering a team talk not just to her players, but to us all.

Let's go, New York City! ...

This is crazy. This is absolutely insane. I'm at such a loss for words. I mean I'll find them, don't worry. ...

First and foremost: my teammates. Just shout-out to the teammates.... This group is so resilient, is so tough, has such a sense of humour, is just so bad-ass. Like, there's nothing – *nothing* – that can faze this group. We're chillin'. We've got tea sipping. We've got celebrations. We have pink hair and purple hair. We have tattoos and dreadlocks. We've got white girls and black girls, and everything in between. Straight girls and gay girls.

I couldn't be more proud to be a co-captain with Carli and Alex for this team. It's my absolute honour to lead this team out on the field. There's no other place that I would rather be – even in the presidential race. I'm busy, I'm sorry.

To the staff: to the coaching staff, the technical staff, to the medical staff, to the support staff, to the massage therapists, to the videographers, to the chef, to our security, to our media people – thank you so much. You make our jobs so easy. We don't have to focus on anything other than what we have to do on the field. Thank you for that. [...]

To the NYPD, to the fire department here, to everyone who made this happen, thank you so much. This would not be possible without everyone. We really do appreciate all that it takes to shut down the biggest, best city in the world. For the biggest, best team in the world. Thank you for that. It means the world to us.

I think I'll just end with this. This is my charge to everyone: we have to be better. We have to love more, hate less. We've got to listen more and talk less. We've got to know that this is everybody's responsibility: every single person here, every single person who is not here, every single person who doesn't want to be here, every single person who agrees and doesn't agree – it's our responsibility to make this world a better place.

I think this team does an incredible job of taking that on our shoulders and understanding the position that we have and the platform that we have within this world. Yes, we play sports. Yes, we play soccer. Yes, we're female athletes. But we're so much more than that.

You're so much more than that. You're more than a fan. You're more than someone who just supports sports. You're more than someone who tunes in every four years. You're someone who walks these streets every single day. You interact with your community every single day.

How do you make your community better? How do you make the people around you better? Your family? Your closest friends, the ten people closest to you, the twenty people closest to you, the hundred people closest to you? It's every single person's responsibility.

There's been so much contention in these last years. I've been a victim of that. I've been a perpetrator of that. But to the federation, sorry for some of the things I said.

Not all of the things.

But it's time to come together. This conversation is at the next step. We have to collaborate. It takes everybody. This is my charge to everybody: do what you can. Do what you have to do. Step outside yourself. Be more. Be better. Be bigger than you've ever been before.

If this team is any representation of what you can be when you do that, please take this as an example. This group is incredible. We took so much on our shoulders to be here today, to celebrate with you today. And we did it with a smile. So do the same for us. Please. I ask you.

ROSIE DUFFIELD

'Sometimes There Are No Bruises'

HOUSE OF COMMONS

October 2019

As Labour MP Rosie Duffield made this speech in the House of Commons, MPs on all sides fell silent, catching the gravity and sensitivity of her words as she started to describe the harrowing reality of domestic abuse and coercive control. I remember the heartbreaking moment, sitting on the benches near her, when I realized that Rosie was talking about herself. This incredibly brave speech is one of the most personal and powerful I have ever heard.

It was important in so many ways. Never have I heard a clearer description of how pernicious and dangerous coercive control can be. As Rosie explains how 'sometimes there are no bruises', she takes us with her on a journey – of meeting someone, of romantic gestures and words of affirmation, of the hopes and dreams associated with those early days, through the subtle forms of criticism and control as they start to appear and raise alarms, and ultimately to overt aggression and abuse, whether it's emotional, financial or physical. She bravely chronicles her own feelings of self-doubt, confusion, exhaustion, fear and the growing sense of danger.

For people across the country suffering under coercive control, Rosie put into words a tormented experience of escalating bullying and abuse which can diminish a person and leave them feeling trapped, isolated and helpless. Her speech had a remarkable impact. Hundreds of thousands of people watched it online. In the week that followed, Rosie received thousands of emails from people in similar situations.

By speaking out about her own experience, Rosie also exploded the myth that domestic abuse only happens to those who are weak or those who are poor. If it can happen to someone who has become an elected Member of Parliament, helping decide the laws of the land, it can happen to anyone. As she explained, she wanted to show that 'domestic violence has many faces, and the faces of those who survive it are varied, too'. Her decision to share her story was powerful evidence that the perpetrators don't discriminate based on who you are, where you're from, how much you earn or the job you do.

What she did was also extremely brave. Domestic abuse can be difficult to discuss with a close friend, let alone on such a public stage. Like any woman politician, Rosie has had painful experiences of being publicly targeted by haters and vilified online for the smallest of things. The vulnerability that inevitably comes with being in the public eye can often make politicians put up higher walls to defend their privacy. Rosie tore those walls down in order to help others.

She later told me how daunting it was, and how she had written the speech so that she could still change her mind at the last minute and make it sound like she was drawing on the experience of a constituent or a friend rather than her own. And that even while delivering the speech, it was only when she reached the sentence about introducing him to her party leader that she knew she had passed the point of no return. That tussle in Rosie's own mind between silence and speaking out is part of what makes the speech so piercing.

It is very hard to hear a friend recount such difficult experiences, but all of us on the Labour benches were immensely proud of Rosie that day – as you can see if you watch it, from the way we all tearfully rally around her at the end. It is that feeling of being supported, protected and believed by friends, family and colleagues that Rosie wants to impart to anyone listening, when she calls at the end of the speech for others to reach out because 'we will be there and we will hold your hand'.

But more than anything, this is an inspiring and defiant speech – these are the words of a woman who has come through abuse and shown incredible strength, reassuring others who might be suffering with warming words about the ability to overcome, and the slow but certain relief and gradual return to happiness once the ordeal is over and life can be resumed.

Rosie described in an interview that when you're bullied, you can't think of the right words – 'you're not eloquent. I would misspeak, stutter'. Abuse is a form of silencing. But with this speech, Rosie broke the silence. She used her voice to reclaim power for herself and for countless others too.

If anyone reading Rosie's speech is in a similar situation and needs help or support, please call the National Domestic Abuse Helpline, which is open 24 hours a day, on 0808 2000 247. You are not alone.

So what is domestic violence or abuse, and where do we get our ideas about it from? Often we see the same images and stereotypes on TV: housing estates, working-class families, drunk men coming home from the pub, women surrounded by children, and a sequence of shouting, followed by immediate physical violence or assault. But soap opera scenes tend to focus on only one or two aspects of a much bigger and more complex picture.

Domestic violence has many faces, and the faces of those who survive it are varied, too. There are 650 MPs in this place – 650 human beings. Statistically, it is highly likely that some of us here will have directly experienced an abusive relationship, and we are just as likely as anyone else to have grown up in a violent household.

Abuse is not just about noticeable physical signs. Sometimes there are no bruises. Abuse is very often all about control and power; it is about abusers making themselves feel big, or biggest. But that is not how they present themselves. It is not how they win your heart. It is not how they persuade you to meet them for a coffee, then go to a gig, and then spend an evening snuggled up in front of a movie at their place.

When they ask you out they do not present their rage, and do not tell you that while they like the idea of strong, independent, successful women, they do not like the reality. They do not threaten, criticize, control, yell or exert their physical strength in an increasingly frightening way – not yet. Not at the start. Not when they think you are sweet, funny and gorgeous. Not when they want to impress you. Not when they turn up to only your third date with chocolate, and then jewellery. Not when they meet your friends, your parents or the leader of your political party. They do not do any of that then.

It is only later, when the door to your home is locked, that you really start to learn what power and control look and feel like. That is when you learn that 'I'll always look after you', 'I'll never let you go', and 'You're mine for life' can sound menacing, and are used as a warning over and over again. It is when the ring is on your finger that the mask can start to slip, and the promises sound increasingly like threats. It is then that you spend twelve or more hours at work longing to see the person you love, only to find that on the walk or Tube journey home they refuse to speak a single, solitary word to you.

Eventually, at home, they will find a way to let you know which particular sin you have apparently committed: your dress was too short, the top you wore in the Chamber was too low-cut, or you did not respond to a message immediately.

It starts slowly: a few emotional knocks, alternated with romantic gushes and promises of everlasting love, which leave you reeling, confused, spinning around in an ever-changing but always hyper-alert state, not knowing what mood or message awaits you. You tell yourself to be less sensitive, less emotional, to stop over-analysing every little thing. Ignore the moods – he never stops saying he adores you, right? All seems good again.

A whole week goes by: a week of summer-evening walks home and maybe a drink on the way. A long weekend is booked and organized as a surprise while you are at work. The journey there is full of promise and promises – time away, alone together in a place away from stress – but then it starts.

In a strange city, his face changes in a way you are starting to know and dread, in a way that says you need to stay calm, silent and very careful. He goes for a walk. You sit in your hotel room and wait. You read a city guide and plan which sights you want to visit, mentally packing a day full of fun. But he seems to have another agenda. He doesn't want you to leave the room. He has paid a lot of money and you need to pay him your full attention. You are expected to do as you are told, and you know for certain what that means – so you do exactly as you are told.

In the months that follow, those patterns continue: reward, punishment, promises of happily ever after alternated with abject rage, menace, silent treatment and coercive control; financial abuse and control; a point-blank refusal to disclose his salary or earnings; an assumption and insistence on it being OK to live in your home without contributing a single penny, as bills continue to pile up; a refusal to work, as your salary is great and public knowledge; the false promises to start paying some specific bills, which you discover months later remain unpaid; and the slow but sure disappearance of any kindness, respect or loving behaviour.

You get to the stage where you are afraid to go home. After fifteen hours at work, you spend another hour on the phone to your mum or a close friend, trembling, a shadow of your usual self. You answer the phone, and the sheer nastiness and rage tell you not to go home at all. So you leave work with your best friend, exhausted and shaking, and buy a toothbrush on the way, knowing that the verbal abuse followed by silent refusal to speak at all will be a hundred times worse tomorrow.

Every day is emotionally exhausting. You are working in a job you love but putting on a brave face and pretending all is good, fine – wonderful, in fact. Then the pretence and the public face start to drop completely: being yelled at in the car with the windows down, no attempt to hide controlling behaviour during constituency engagements, humiliation and embarrassment now added to the permanent trepidation and constant hurt and pain.

It is impossible to comprehend that this is the person who tells his family how much he loves you and longs to make you his wife. But the mask has slipped for good, and questions are starting. Excuses are given to worried friends, concerned family members and colleagues who have started to notice. One night, after more crying and being constantly verbally abused because you suggested he pay a bit towards your new sofa, you realize you've reached the end and you simply cannot endure this for another day or week, and certainly not for the rest of your life.

Having listened intently for two whole weeks to the sound of his morning shower, timing the routine until you know it off by heart, you summon up the courage to take his front-door keys from his bag. You have tried everything else on earth and know for certain, 100 per cent, what awaits you that night if you do not act today. Heart banging, you hide them carefully and creep back into bed, praying he won't discover what you have done.

You know for certain what will happen if he does. You know an apology will not follow. You know for sure it will be because of what you have done and that it is all your fault. He leaves for the gym, telling you how much he adores you. He tells you to remember that you will always be his. He kisses you lovingly, as though there have not been months of verbal abuse, threats and incidents he knows you will never disclose. He tells you he will bring something nice home for dinner.

Sure enough, the next few days and weeks are a total hell – texts and calls and yelling: 'You've locked me out like a dog', 'No one treats me that way', 'This is the last thing you will ever do'. You cry, you grieve for your destroyed dreams, you try to heal, you ignore the emails from wedding companies, but it is like withdrawal, and it takes six months.

But one day you notice that you're smiling, that it's OK to laugh, and that it's been a week or two since the daily sobbing stopped. You realize you are allowed to be happy. You dare to relax and you dare to start to feel free. You realize it is not your fault and that he is now left alone with his rage and narcissism. You dare to start dating someone, and you realize that you have survived, but the brightest and most precious thing of all is realizing that you are loved and believed by friends, family and colleagues who believe in you and support you.

So if anyone is watching and needs a friend, please reach out, if it is safe to do so, and please talk to any of us, because we will be there and we will hold your hand.

QUEEN ELIZABETH II

'We Will Meet Again'

ADDRESS TO THE NATION, WINDSOR

April 2020

This televised address by Queen Elizabeth II during the COVID-19 crisis was unlike any other Royal speech in history. It was delivered to the nation in an unprecedented lockdown – not at war or going off to battle, but amidst a health emergency on a scale we have never seen in modern times. Unlike the rallying battle cries of Boudica and Elizabeth I, this was not the speech of a warrior queen. Rather, it was a moving and compassionate tribute to the spirit of a nation, to sturdy resilience, social duty and quiet strength – to the attributes we tend to associate with the Queen herself, but most importantly to the qualities we would need in order to get through the adversity ahead.

I watched the speech from our sitting room. Never had things felt more uncertain, or the country more anxious. We were two weeks into lockdown. Thousands of people had already died. Thousands more were being rushed into hospital unable to breathe. Schools were closed, exams called off. Shops and factories, offices, pubs, clubs and restaurants stood empty. Medical operations were cancelled. Courts were suspended. All competitive sport had stopped. Churches, mosques and synagogues had closed their doors. Weddings were postponed and mourners were barred from funerals. Parliament was shut. Within hours of the Queen's speech, the government announced that the Prime Minister had become so ill with COVID-19, he had been taken into hospital. The following day, he went into intensive care. Everything we normally took for granted, every institution, every trace of normality, was suspended or under immense strain.

In the middle of the national crisis was a void. While the public response to the crisis had been strong – people staying home and making sacrifices in the national interest, communities rallying round to help the most vulnerable – you could feel the need for someone or something to embody the determination and resilience of a nation coming together in the face of a shared threat. We saw it in the overwhelming support for the NHS, the doorstep clapping and singing for our carers every Thursday evening – a fierce need we all felt not just to thank and applaud the bravery and commitment of staff on the frontline of the crisis, but also to find national institutions and symbols that could draw us together in collective endeavour at an incredibly difficult time. That evening, in the absence of any rallying voice from the government to unite around, we also found it in the words of the Queen.

She captured a moment of history, a country yearning to come together just as we needed to stay apart, and her words evoked a sense of common purpose in the face of the unknown. The Queen recognized the way that the NHS and children's painted rainbows had become powerful embodiments of a national spirit, and her words are inclusive, drawing everyone in, 'all faiths and none', the essential workers and those staying home. And it reflected what was happening across the country too; in my constituency, we set up community hubs to deliver food and medicines, primary-school children wrote cards for care-home residents, the local Burberry factory started manufacturing NHS gowns, and people everywhere were checking in on neighbours and making each other smile on video calls.

At the heart of the speech, the Queen's invocation of wartime sentiment is powerful for its simplicity and authenticity. As she describes her first ever radio broadcast in 1940 when, as a child, she and her sister had spoken to children who had been evacuated, she brings to mind the even greater sacrifices that families have made in generations past to keep each other safe. Most powerful of all is the way she draws on that history to create a sense of shared national purpose:

The attributes of self-discipline, of quiet good-humoured resolve and of fellow-feeling still characterize this country. The pride in who we are is not a part of our past, it defines our present and our future.

Only the Queen could have made this speech. It was the voice of a 96-year-old with unparalleled perspective on our history, a monarch who has been a constant presence through most of our lives, the embodiment of stability, resilience and history just when the world had turned upside down.

At the time of writing this, just a few months later, both the Queen's speech and that moment of yearning for national unity in the face of crisis already seem like they were a long time ago, and things feel fractured once again. We have passed the first phase of the virus, and we know not yet what further challenges lie ahead. In this strange time, I suspect some who watched it may since have forgotten how resonant the Queen's speech and words were on that first dark April weekend. But she captured an intense and difficult historic moment and that final line is incredibly poignant and enduring, drawing on the iconic wartime song to reassure us that we too will come through this and not be forever apart: 'We will meet again.'

I am speaking to you at what I know is an increasingly challenging time. A time of disruption in the life of our country: a disruption that has brought grief to some, financial difficulties to many, and enormous changes to the daily lives of us all.

I want to thank everyone on the NHS frontline, as well as care workers and those carrying out essential roles, who selflessly continue their day-to-day duties outside the home in support of us all. I am sure the nation will join me in assuring you that what you do is appreciated and every hour of your hard work brings us closer to a return to more normal times.

I also want to thank those of you who are staying at home, thereby helping to protect the vulnerable and sparing many families the pain already felt by those who have lost loved ones. Together we are tackling this disease, and I want to reassure you that if we remain united and resolute, then we will overcome it.

I hope in the years to come everyone will be able to take pride in how they responded to this challenge. And those who come after us will say that the Britons of this generation were as strong as any; that the attributes of self-discipline, of quiet good-humoured resolve and of fellow-feeling still characterize this country. The pride in who we are is not a part of our past, it defines our present and our future. The moments when the United Kingdom has come together to applaud its care and essential workers will be remembered as an expression of our national spirit; and its symbol will be the rainbows drawn by children.

Across the Commonwealth and around the world, we have seen heart-warming stories of people coming together to help others, be it through delivering food parcels and medicines, checking on neighbours, or converting businesses to help the relief effort. And though self-isolating may at times be hard, many people of all faiths, and of none, are discovering that it presents an opportunity to slow down, pause and reflect, in prayer or meditation.

It reminds me of the very first broadcast I made, in 1940, helped by my sister. We, as children, spoke from here at Windsor to children who had been evacuated from their homes and sent away for their own safety. Today, once again, many will feel a painful sense of separation from their loved ones. But now, as then, we know deep down that it is the right thing to do.

While we have faced challenges before, this one is different. This time we join with all nations across the globe in a common endeavour, using the great advances of science and our instinctive compassion to heal. We will succeed – and that success will belong to every one of us.

We should take comfort that while we may have more still to endure, better days will return: we will be with our friends again; we will be with our families again; we will meet again.

But for now, I send my thanks and warmest good wishes to you all.

”

ACKNOWLEDGEMENTS

Thanks go first to all the women whose speeches are included in this book – for their words, ideas and courage in speaking out. I hope this helps more women to follow them.

This book of speeches wouldn't have happened without three brilliant women: Amy Richards, with whom I first discussed the idea four years ago, and who pushed me to start it; Beth Gardiner-Smith who gave me the first suggestions for speeches to include; and Natasha Collett who made it happen this year, by keeping me on track with research, drafting and creative ideas. I look forward to listening to their speeches in years to come. Thank you to them and also to the very many friends, colleagues and particularly my long-suffering office teams who have helped me write and deliver speeches in my own last-minute kind of way over many years. You know who you are.

Huge thanks go to Mike Harpley, Kat Ailes and the team at Atlantic who believed in this project enough both to set me deadlines to make it happen and to be endlessly patient when Brexit chaos meant they were all broken. The beautiful illustrations by the brilliant Anna Higgie make the speeches come alive. Thank you to Sophie Lambert at C&W who kept everything running smoothly.

Thank you to those – especially Labour women MPs – who suggested great speeches to include, but more importantly who have shown me and each other such friendship and solidarity when we have faced threats for speaking out. At a time when tensions are rising, thanks go to those on all sides of politics who, whatever our disagreements, try to show each other respect and kindness.

But most thanks go to my family and friends. To my Mum and Dad who gave me the confidence to make speeches and supported our whole family while I was making them; to my sister Nichola and brother David and their families, and to Alison and Phil and family who put up with me writing introductions during our summer holiday this year.

Ed and I have spent over twenty years commenting on each other's speeches, rewriting each other's jokes, practising them together and cheerily dissecting other people's speeches at weddings, receptions or conferences. Speeches (and most things) are always more fun when Ed is involved.

Meanwhile our children Ellie, Joel and Maddy have endured endless speeches through the years, as babies in slings, toddlers holding my hand, restless seven-year-olds and bored teenagers sitting at the back.

So more than anything else, thank you to Ed, Ellie, Joel and Maddy for supporting me, defending me (especially against each other) and for being by far the best feminists I know.

CREDITS

The speeches in this book are taken from the following sources, all by permission of the speaker unless stated otherwise. Every effort has been made to trace the copyright holders of the speeches published in this book. The editor and publisher apologize if any material has been included without permission or without the appropriate acknowledgement, and would be glad to be told of anyone who has not been consulted. All those not listed are out of copyright.

A note on style: where an ellipsis within square brackets is used in quoted speech it denotes a substantial amount of missing text, e.g. a paragraph or more; where an ellipsis is used on its own it denotes a small amount of missing text within a paragraph or sentence.

Diane Abbott, 'We Will Not Rest' (Houses of Parliament, UK, April 2019) by kind permission of Diane Abbott.

Chimamanda Ngozi Adichie, *We Should All Be Feminists*, Copyright © 2012, 2014, Chimamanda Ngozi Adichie, used by permission of The Wylie Agency (UK) Limited.

Maya Angelou, 'On the Pulse of Morning' from *And Still I Rise: A Book of Poems* by Maya Angelou, copyright © 1978 by Maya Angelou. Used by permission of Random House, an imprint and division of Penguin Random House LLC. All rights reserved.

Jacinda Ardern, 'They Are Us' (New Zealand Parliament, March 2019).

Benazir Bhutto, 'The Ethos of Islam is Equality Between the Sexes' speech by Benazir Bhutto. Copyright © 1995, Benazir Bhutto, used by permission of The Wylie Agency (UK) Limited.

Barbara Castle, 'The Red Light Has Gone On' (Labour Party Conference, September 2000) by kind permission of David Higham Associates.

Marie Colvin, 'Someone Has to Go There' (London, November 2010), by kind permission of the Marie Colvin estate.

Jo Cox, 'More in Common' (Houses of Parliament, UK, June 2015).

Rosie Duffield, 'Sometimes There Are No Bruises' (Houses of Parliament, UK, October 2019), by kind permission of Rosie Duffield.

Queen Elizabeth II, 'We Will Meet Again' (Windsor Castle, UK, April 2020), Crown Copyright © 2020, used under Open Government Licence.

Ellen DeGeneres, 'I Know Who I Am' (Tulane University, May 2009) by permission of ICM Partners.

Alison Drake, 'Get Up There and Get At It' (Castleford Heritage Trust, September 2010).

Julia Gillard, 'He Needs a Mirror' (Australian Parliament, October 2012).

Harriet Harman, 'Parliament Must Lead by Example' (Houses of Parliament, UK, July 2014) by kind permission of Harriet Harman.

Eva Kor, 'A Message of Hope and Healing' (June 2001) by kind permission of Eva Kor/CANDLES Holocaust Museum and Education Center.

Kavita Krishnan, 'Freedom Without Fear' (All India Progressive Women's Association Protest, December 2013), by kind permission of Kavita Krishnan. Translation by Nishita Jha.

Audre Lorde, 'There Are So Many Silences to Be Broken' from *I Am Your Sister: Collected and Unpublished Writings of Audre Lorde*, ed. Rudolph P. Byrd, Johnnetta B. Cole, and Beverly Guy-Sheftall (Oxford: Oxford UP, 2009) by kind permission of Abner Stein.

Wangari Maathai, 'A World of Beauty and Wonder' (December 2004) © The Nobel Foundation 2004.

Lilit Martirosyan, 'We Are Making History Today' (Armenian National Assembly, April 2019).

Theresa May, 'Modernizing the Conservative Party' (Conservative Party Conference, October 2002) by kind permission of the office of Theresa May.

Angela Merkel, 'A Door Suddenly Opened' (US Congress, November 2009), by kind permission of the office of Angela Merkel.

Lupita Nyong'o, 'Being Beautiful Inside', *Essence: Black Women in Hollywood Conference* (California, February 2014) by kind permission of Creative Arts Agency.

Michelle Obama, 'When They Go Low, We Go High' (Democratic National Convention, July 2016).

Alexandria Ocasio-Cortez, 'Today I Rise' (US Congress, January 2019) by kind permission of the Office of Alexandria Ocasio-Cortez.

Joan O'Connell, 'The Promise of a Dream' (TUC Report, 1968) by kind permission of Trades Union Congress (TUC).

Joanne O'Riordan, 'No Limbs No Limits' ('Girls in Technology' Conference, April 2012).

Megan Rapinoe, 'Be Better, Be Bigger' (New York, July 2019), by kind permission of Wasserman Media Group.

Manal al-Sharif, 'Driving for Freedom' (Oslo, May 2012), by kind permission of Manal al-Sharif.

Donna Strickland, 'Physics is Fun' (Nobel Banquet, December 2018) © The Nobel Foundation 2018.

Margaret Thatcher, 'The Lady's Not for Turning' (Conservative Party Conference, 10 October 1980). Copyright estate of Lady Thatcher, extracts reprinted with permission from the text in www.margaretthatcher.org.

Greta Thunberg, 'Let's Start Acting' (R20 Austrian World Summit, May 2019) by kind permission of Daniel Donner on behalf of the Thunberg family.

Emma Watson, 'HeForShe' (UN Headquarters, September 2014) by kind permission of Prosper PR Limited.

Malala Yousafzai, 'Let Us Pick Up Our Books and Our Pens' (UN General Assembly, July 2013) by kind permission of Curtis Brown UK.

Permissions cleared courtesy of Swift Permissions
swiftpermissions@gmail.com

ENDNOTES

1 https://www.thesojournertruth project.com/

2 https://www.theguardian.com/ artanddesign/2006/sep/21/art1

3 http://www.charlottenewson.com/ women-like-you/

4 https://www.oxforddnb.com/view/ 10.1093/ref:odnb/9780198614128. 001.0001/odnb-9780198614128-e- 35376?rskey=EGHW5f&result=1

5 https://www.oxforddnb.com/view/ 10.1093/ref:odnb/9780198614128. 001.0001/odnb-9780198614128-e- 35376?rskey=EGHW5f&result=1

6 https://www.bbc.co.uk/news/ business-30112814

7 https://www.poetryfoundation.org/ poets/audre-lorde

8 http://s18.middlebury.edu/ AMST0325A/Lorde_The_Masters_ Tools.pdf

9 https://www.theguardian.com/ books/2014/may/28/maya-angelou

10 https://www.latimes.com/archives/ la-xpm-1993-01-17-op-1952-story. html

11 https://commonslibrary.parliament. uk/insights/the-history-and- geography-of-women-mps-since- 1918-in-numbers/

12 https://candlesholocaustmuseum. org/eva-kor/her-story/her-story.html/ title/read-about-eva-and-miriam- after-the-war

13 https://www.gov.uk/government/ speeches/statement-from-the-new- prime-minister-theresa-may

14 https://www.bbc.co.uk/news/ election-2017-40192060

15 https://www.greenbeltmovement. org/wangari-maathai

16 https://www.un.org/esa/forests/ news/2011/09/un-pays-tribute-to- late-environmentalist-and-nobel- laureate-wangari-maathai/index. html

17 https://edition.cnn.com/2019/08/02/ middleeast/saudi-women-travel- passport-intl-hnk/index.html

18 https://www.nytimes. com/2017/06/09/opinion/sunday/ saudi-arabia-women-driving-ban. html

19 https://time.com/5567330/saudi- arabia-women-rights-drive/

20 https://www.amnesty.org/en/ latest/news/2020/03/saudi-arabia- womens-rights-campaigner-loujain- alhathloul-due-in-court/

21 https://www.telegraph.co.uk/travel/ destinations/oceania/articles/Julia- Gillards-small-breasts-huge-thighs- on-opposition-partys-fundraiser- menu/

22 https://www.abc.net.au/news/ specials/rudd-returns/2013-06-26/ julia-gillard-speaks-about-defeat/ 4783950

23 https://www.ted.com/talks/
chimamanda_adichie_the_danger_
of_a_single_story

24 https://www.opendemocracy.net/en/
5050/women-demand-freedom-not-
surveillance/

25 https://www.theguardian.com/
politics/2014/feb/09/kavita-
krishnan-communist-india-accused-
minister-free-sex

26 https://www.indiatoday.in/india/
story/five-women-raped-everyday-
in-delhi-last-year-police-1427501-
2019-01-10

27 https://www.washingtonpost.
com/news/arts-and-entertainment/
wp/2014/03/02/transcript-lupita-
nyongos-emotional-oscars-
acceptance-speech/

28 https://www.nytimes.com/2017/10/
19/opinion/lupita-nyongo-harvey-
weinstein.html

29 Harman, Harriet (2017) *A Woman's
Work*. Penguin

30 https://www.independent.co.uk/
news/people/emma-watson-was-
encouraged-not-to-use-the-word-
feminism-during-un-heforshe-
speech-a6756796.html

31 https://www.theguardian.com/
world/2015/nov/05/malala-
yousafzai-tells-emma-watson-im-a-
feminist-thanks-to-you

32 https://www.standard.co.uk/
showbiz/celebrity-news/emma-
watson-received-threats-after-
opening-pandora-s-box-with-un-
campaign-a3358146.html

33 https://www.iop.org/policy/statistics/
uk-a-levels/gender/page_67095.html

34 https://www.aps.org/programs/
education/statistics/

35 http://www.bbc.com/future/story/
20181008-why-dont-more-women-
dont-win-nobel-prizes-in-science

36 https://www.amnesty.org.uk/press-
releases/diane-abbott-talks-about-
sheer-levels-hatred-she-receives-
online

37 https://www.amnesty.org.uk/press-
releases/diane-abbott-talks-about-
sheer-levels-hatred-she-receives-
online

38 https://www.theyworkforyou.com/
whall/?id=2017-07-12a.151.0

39 https://speakola.com/arts/laverne-
cox-trans-rights-creating-change-
2014

40 https://www.bbc.co.uk/news/uk-
48756370

41 https://www.theguardian.com/
global-development/2019/apr/26/
armenian-mps-call-for-trans-activist-
to-be-burned-alive-after-historic-
speech-lilit-martirosyan

42 https://www.reuters.com/article/
us-armenia-lgbt-politics/armenias-
lgbt-community-still-waits-for-
change-one-year-after-revolution-
idUSKCN1S300H

43 https://www.reuters.com/article/
us-armenia-lgbt-politics/armenias-
lgbt-community-still-waits-for-
change-one-year-after-revolution-
idUSKCN1S300H

44 https://www.bbc.co.uk/newsround/
    47467038

45 https://www.theguardian.com/
    environment/2019/apr/23/greta-
    thunberg-full-speech-to-mps-you-
    did-not-act-in-time

46 https://www.bbc.co.uk/news/uk-
    politics-48126677

47 https://www.independent.co.uk/
    life-style/fashion/womens-world-
    cup-2019-usa-soccer-shirt-bestseller-
    nike-buy-price-a8986481.html

48 https://www.fifa.com/
    womensworldcup/news/fifa-
    womens-world-cup-2019tm-
    watched-by-more-than-1-billion